CONVERSATIONS WITH
ST. FRANCIS

More praise for *Conversations with Saint Francis:*

"Saint Francis comes alive in a fresh, engaging, and exciting way in these pages. James Howell shows us how the words and life of this subversive saint can guide us toward becoming more faithful followers of Jesus in our contemporary context. In our search for a genuine gospel spirituality, we would do well to listen to this ancient voice."

—Trevor Hudson, South African pastor and author of *A Mile In My Shoes, Listen to the Groans,* and *Transforming Discipleship.*

CONVERSATIONS WITH
ST. FRANCIS

JAMES C. HOWELL

Abingdon Press
Nashville

CONVERSATIONS WITH ST. FRANCIS

This book is printed on acid-free paper.

Library of Congress Cataloging-in-Publication Data

Howell, James C., 1955–
    Conversations with Saint Francis / James C. Howell.
        p. cm.
    Includes bibliographical references.
    ISBN 978-0-687-65049-1
    1. Francis, of Assisi, Saint, 1182-1226. I. Title.

    BX4700.F6H645 2008
    271'.302—dc22

                                                    2008002643

Scripture quotations noted KJV are taken from the King James or Authorized Version of the Bible.

Scripture quotations noted RSV are taken from the Revised Standard Version of the Bible, copyright 1952 [2nd edition, 1971] by the Division of Christian Education of the National Council of the Churches of Christ in the United States of America. Used by permission. All rights reserved.

Scripture quotations noted NRSV are taken from the New Revised Standard Version of the Bible, copyright 1989, Division of Christian Education of the National Council of the Churches of Christ in the United States of America. Used by permission. All rights reserved.

Scripture quotations noted NIV are taken from the Holy Bible, NEW INTERNATIONAL VERSION®. Copyright © 1973, 1978, 1984 by International Bible Society. All rights reserved throughout the world. Used by permission of International Bible Society.

Texts from Francis of Assisi: Early Documents, Volume 1: The Saint, Volume 3: The Prophet are used with permission. (Copyright 1999, 2001 Franciscan Institute of St. Bonaventure, NY. Published by New City Press, 202 Cardinal Rd., Hyde Park, NY 12538 [www.newcitypress.com]).

The St. Francis Prayer Book: A Guide to Deepen Your Spiritual Life
By Jon M. Sweeney
©2004 Jon M. Sweeney
Used by permission of Paraclete Press, www.paracletepress.com

Lawrence Cunningham, Francis of Assisi: Performing the Gospel Life © 2004 Wm B. Eerdmans Publishing Company, Grand Rapids, Michigan. Reprinted by permission of the publisher; all rights reserved.

A note about the drawings in this book: After her pilgrimage to Assisi, and seeing the frescoes of the life of Francis in various churches around Italy, Grace Howell sketched the drawings that appear in this book in the style of medieval fresco.

08 09 10 11 12 13 14 15 16 17—10 9 8 7 6 5 4 3 2 1

MANUFACTURED IN THE UNITED STATES OF AMERICA

To Phillip, who first introduced me to Assisi

and

To Ann Spencer, Carey, Courtney, Dana, Dianne, Grace,

Joe, Laura, Mary Catherine, and Sarah,

who made pilgrimage with me

CONTENTS

INTRODUCTION

In October of 1984, I found myself in Rome visiting a friend, a former Methodist pastor who had converted to the Roman Catholic Church and was studying theology in Italy. To me, making such a journey, and knowing a priest there personally, seemed almost chic, a heady delight. Facing a break from his studies, Phillip suggested we take the train to Assisi. Little did I know this junket would forever alter my perspective, my passions, and even my habits. Little did I know I would return there many times, not as a sightseer but as a pilgrim, dragging others along so they might experience my newfound friend, St. Francis.

Sure, I knew a little more about St. Francis than the average person. I had studied the medieval Church in graduate school and understood that the little statues and birdbaths I'd seen adorning flower beds trivialized the immense, revolutionary depth of the saint from Assisi. But I hadn't paid a lot of attention to things Franciscan, neither in my historical studies nor in my private spirituality. I had, in fact, poked fun at a spiritual advisor who had suggested I get to know Francis more personally. A few months before I made that first journey to Assisi, a gang of us Methodist clergy were commanded to appear for a three-day retreat. Not only were there long, anguished swaths of time in which we were not permitted to talk (a herculean effort for a babbler like me). We also were administered the Myers-Briggs personality test. The cynic in me resists such oversimplified categorizing of inner complexities: I mean, what "type" is the guy who cut me off in traffic today?

My graded test paper indicated I was an ENTJ. The diagnosis of how and why ENTJs think and act as they do was way more on target than I cared to acknowledge. Some self-disclosure, some growth in self-awareness, was going on. But then, instead of letting me groove as the ENTJ whom God obviously made me to be, this advisor spoke of my "shadow" side, my opposite, the personality zone where I am uncomfortable—but where I need to stretch if I am to become more whole, more mature, less easily thrown off balance. The opposite of an ENTJ is an ISFP—and then she told me, "St. Francis was an ISFP, you know." I laughed out loud, shook my head, my sarcastic intellect mocking the notion that we can ascertain such a thing across nearly eight full centuries. Little did I know that Francis, that old ISFP, would for the rest of my life (so far!) be precisely the stretch I have desperately needed, eagerly sought, and belatedly found.

SLEEPLESS IN ASSISI

Phillip and I stepped off the train, the station more sparse than I had expected, fixed in the flat plain of Umbria, at the edge of a modern town like most others in Europe. But Phillip pointed east, toward the mountains. There it was, the medieval, terraced, walled city where Francis had grown up, almost hovering above the plain, beckoning us to come. Later I would read what Pope John XXIII had said about this vista: "Assisi is surely a suburb of heaven. Here we are truly at the gates of paradise. Why did God give Assisi this aura of sanctity, almost suspended in the air, which the pilgrim feels almost tangibly? So that men will recognize their creator and recognize each other as brothers."[1]

A taxi hauled us and our things to a lovely pensione, our base for three days of walking, sitting in churches, kneeling in prayer, conversing. I picked up a copy of *The Little Flowers of St. Francis* and read its quaint stories of the saint's life.

At night, despite the comforts of the pensione, I simply could not sleep. I would fall asleep easily, but then I would waken at 1:00 or 2:00 a.m. Although I do not believe I have a mystical bone in my body, and although I generally chuckle in disdain when I hear things like I am about to say, I feel fairly certain that Francis himself was shaking me out of my slumber each night and refused to let me sleep. When he lived in Assisi, he did not sleep much, and his friends reported that he frequently prayed all night long. Was he lurking in this pensione? Was this a getaway for the haunted? Had Francis wakened others in this place?

I do not know. But my life hasn't been the same since. I have returned to Assisi a number of times and have read a decent percentage of what has been published about St. Francis. I've written about him in other books and in articles; he has been the subject of classes I've taught and has appeared in enough sermons to cause my parishioners to surmise I must have gotten stuck back in thirteenth-century Umbria.

My return trips to Assisi have all been provocative, each journey in its own peculiar, delightful way. A few days there with my oldest daughter, Sarah, were deeply moving, and in this book I will share some of the journal entries and poetry she wrote while we were there. In 2007, my colleague Joe Hamby and I hatched the intriguing idea of taking a group of teenagers to Assisi—and I thank God for that flash of insight, which I feel inclined to chalk up to the Spirit. Or perhaps it was Francis himself summoning me from a world away to bring them. We studied the life of Francis and discussed issues like family, clothing, beauty, and vocation in preparation for the journey.

So I found myself in Assisi once more, and with a group of teenagers, most of them having grown up as privileged as Francis himself. I watched them carefully to see what would happen to them. Would they feel the presence of Francis? Or would the young women recognize Francis's younger friend Clare? Would this be mere sightseeing, or something richer, a defining moment in their lives? Might one or two throw away all, or even fragments of the privileged life they could easily enjoy, and gravitate toward sainthood?

Day by day we walked where Francis walked. At the climax of several arduous climbs we found rocks, caves, masonry joined to natural stone, modestly marked in Italian or occasionally English with signs basically declaring "Francis slept here" or "Francis prayed here." We hiked four kilometers up to the Eremo delle Carceri, the unspeakably beautiful hermitage looming above Assisi where Francis prayed. We traipsed around the Rieti valley and saw a small red cross Francis painted inside a stone chapel, and the spectacular sanctuary at Greccio where the saint orchestrated history's first live nativity. We even pressed far north to LaVerna where Francis was literally wounded by God with the stigmata, which we will explore later in this book.

Everywhere we went, these remarkable teenagers and I looked, pointed, experienced, conversed, reflected. In the evenings after dinner we delved more deeply into what we had seen together, and then we held hands and prayed; we sensed Francis standing in that circle with us. This pilgrimage has heightened my sense of community with the saint, and the thoughts of my young friends will appear in several chapters.

THE CONVERSATION CONTINUES

On that first junket to Assisi years earlier, I wanted the experience to linger with me; I wanted to have Francis with me during the night when I was no longer in the pensione but was back home. So I purchased a handful of icons: the serene Cimabue with the unforgettably gentle face of Francis, the Romanesque crucifix that miraculously spoke to Francis, posters of the Giotto frescoes capturing dramatic moments in his life. These now hang in my home, in the den, bathroom, and bedroom, and in my office. My daughter Grace interpreted some of these frescoes, and her sketches appear in the pages of this book.

Funny thing about icons. For a long time I thought of them as mnemonic devices to call to mind my role models. I see Francis, so I try to be a little bit more like Francis. But now the icons feel different to me. I see Francis, and it seems he is looking back at me. The icon is like some previously unnoticed window into heaven. I believe that the saints—Francis, my grandparents, and a holy host of others represented pictorially in my living spaces—

are watching me, observing my life, raising an eyebrow now and then, asking a few questions. At times I am embarrassed and think seriously about draping a towel over Francis or the crucifix. But then I let the conversation happen. And it is good, and helpful, and I find myself drawn a little bit closer to the Jesus whom Francis knew so intimately.

I want to invite you into this same conversation. We will ask some questions, the hard ones that matter, and we will see what Francis has to say. We cannot submit queries to him the way you do with the tech help people on your computer. After all, Francis lived eight hundred years ago, and scholars still labor over the best way to disentangle fancy from reality. But I will try, as faithfully and thoroughly as possible, to weigh who Francis was, what he said and wrote, what his admirers (and detractors!) thought about him, and puzzle out some answers to our questions. Not surprisingly, our answers will feel like renewed, reshaped questions coming right back at us. Francis can be known. He can be befriended. He can still speak across the centuries to me and to you.

And to our world. It is wrong to read Francis as a catalyst for me and my private spirituality. Francis was a soldier, he traveled the known world; he labored diligently to renew peace for all God's creation, for all people everywhere. There are undeniable social and political implications that will inevitably emerge as we converse with this saint whose God was too big, too loving, to be confined to the narrowly focused inner life of piety.

A LIFE REDIRECTED

Perhaps the first question I'd want to ask Francis would be something like this: How did you do it? Were you real? How much of your story really happened? And I'm asking because I am wondering how *I* might do it: could I somehow grab a share of the life you had? The marvel in Francis's story is that all he did seems entirely doable—but then, at the same time, ridiculously impossible. As I survey the bare facts of his life, it all seems so manageably simple, and yet unquestionably what happened was nothing short of miraculous.

I can identify with Francis. I feel drawn in to his story, the contours of which are intriguing, dramatic, strangely modern. Growing up, Francis was virtually a pop icon around Assisi. Baptized with the name John (Giovanni), he elicited the nickname Francis (Francesco), meaning "Frenchy." His father, Pietro Bernardone, was a dealer in exotic fabric, and his business took him to France regularly. Francis learned French troubadour songs and affected French manners. Mix in the rising wealth of his family, and we find a wickedly popular young man, a knight on the prowl, the focus of fawning attention.

He was a hip spendthrift, flinging his money about with abandon, buying the coolest fashions, eating and carousing lavishly. But he was not a boor: he cultivated superb manners. Somehow these personality traits—gracious courtesy, reckless spending, and an ability to party with abandon—were not erased by God when Francis was converted. How fascinating: instead of squashing his worldly life, God seemed to revel in Francis's giftedness; God took Francis's politeness, his profligacy, and his inclination to celebrate and redirected them toward holy ends. Or perhaps these traits of being kind and mannerly, keeping the pocketbook open and flowing, ready at any moment to throw a party: isn't this what God made Francis—and you and me—for?

Francis became a soldier, but was badly injured in a war with neighboring Perugia. Convalescing, he dreamed bizarre dreams, perhaps from a fever, or perhaps the visions were from God. He became restless and turned to the Church, praying almost desperately in the little broken-down stone church called San Damiano. Like a toddler finding his legs, Francis became even more generous with his worldly goods, until his father sued him and shattered their family.

Other men were vacuumed into the vortex of this popular young man's spirituality. They moved out of the safe, walled, prosperous city into the valley to live on a pig farm with the poorest of the poor. Francis traveled, preached, dazzled crowds with the directness of his speech and the startling simplicity of his life with God.

He wept much, over Christ's suffering and the agonies he found among the poor. His health deteriorated, and finally he died the night of October 3, in the year 1226. So evident was his sanctity that within two years he was canonized as a saint by Pope Gregory IX, who had been Francis's pastor years earlier. By then his revolutionary way of being a Christian had spread all over Europe, the friars (meaning "brothers") numbering tens of thousands.

Henri Nouwen once asked, "Who will be the St. Francis of our day?"[2] Who indeed? Maybe instead of this daunting question, we should speak with Francis and ask, "Who will I be today? Who might we become in these days?" The answers will probably be utterly simple and brilliantly miraculous. Let the conversation begin.

A WORD ON SOURCES AND METHOD

How do we know what we know about Francis? As I write up this conversation, how persnickety should I try to be about historical accuracy? Let me confess that, although I was trained to care about these matters, I don't want us to get lost in the sifting of sources and scholarly perspectives on them, although once in a while the reliability of sources will need to surface.

Everyone who has written anything about Francis, from back in the Middle Ages up through our century, has some kind of agenda; I know I do. The fact that early biographers fawned over Francis without asking too many questions, and the way they exaggerated things out of love for him: to me, this is lovely, this is part of the story, this is God's poetic license designed to speak to us. Part of the charm of Francis is that so many legends did gravitate toward him. This doesn't happen to you or me, does it?

But if you are interested, here are a few basics. St. Bonaventure wrote an account of St. Francis's life in 1263. Once it was approved by the Franciscan Order, a mandate was issued that all previous biographies of the saint should be destroyed. The poor Franciscans were struggling to get themselves organized, so the publication of a single, focused account struck many as a good idea.

Fortunately, copies of earlier sources were preserved. So we have the first narrative of Francis's life, penned by Thomas of Celano—who knew Francis personally and wrote about him beginning in the year 1228. The pope, Gregory IX, who had been a friend of Francis, ordered this biography be written to support the process of elevating Francis to sainthood. Thomas revised his work a few years later, although the revision begins to feel long-winded and not as razor sharp. We have other early stories, with intriguing titles: "The Anonymous of Perugia," "The Legend of the Three Companions," and "The Mirror of Perfection." A poetic reflection on Francis's life by Henri d'Avranches dates to just six years after the saint's death.

Scholars, like private eyes, sort through the evidence and try to discern when the various authors are pressing their agenda and bending the facts a bit, and when we sense we're face-to-face with Francis[3]—no easy task, since he lived eight centuries ago. I have learned much from properly trained scholars who have written on Francis: Jacques Dalarun, Chiara Frugoni, Michael Robson, Lawrence Cunningham, Joan Mueller, and others. The new three-volume edition of what Francis wrote and what the early Franciscans wrote about him (*Francis of Assisi: Early Documents*) is invaluable.

But I have learned perhaps more from writers whose project is like mine—to discover a living Francis today, to be discovered by Francis today. Murray Bodo's books are all wise, and the superb *The Sun & Moon Over Assisi* by Gerard Thomas Straub is hard to beat. My dream and prayer for my own book is that its contents will be accurate enough historically and at the same time personally truthful enough that you, reader, will find something useful and trustworthy in its pages.

CHAPTER 1

THE WILL OF GOD

If you are the kind of person who reads a book like this, if you wonder about God and the meaning and purpose of your life, if you are at all like me, then you really want to know: what is the will of God? And specifically, what is God's will for me? The intensity of the question rises and falls, depending on the vagaries of life.

But how do you know? I have taken many stabs at divining God's will, although a few times I have felt like a cowboy out on the parched prairie meandering about with a forked stick, desperately thirsty under cloudless skies, yearning for some slight tug that would set me to shoveling for underground water.

The first time I was in Assisi, as powerful as my sense of Francis's presence was, somehow I missed his answer to this most crucial question. What is God's will? Perhaps I wasn't ready to know or even to ask. Maybe I was (and still am?) the kind of person who is too easily distracted, or maybe I'm just plain slow.

But in preparation for my second visit, I read the story of another slow learner's junket to Assisi. Gerard Thomas Straub was a producer of soap operas (like *General Hospital*), an atheist in Hollywood, who through a serpentine twist of circumstances wound up in Assisi—on a chance remark from a priest from whom he was really seeking a restaurant recommendation. The visit changed his life and his career, and I clutched the coattails of his transformation as I read his memoir, *The Sun and Moon Over Assisi*.

Francis would love Straub: a cynic, a worldly guy, all about fashion, style, connections with people who are cool—just like Francis during his early years when he finally began to ask, *What is God's will?* Gulping down his story in huge chunks, I stumbled on what I had missed years earlier, right there on page 467: a prayer, the very words Francis prayed. With my pen I began to underline, then I drew a big circle around it, then with a rush of urgency I sketched a sizable arrow pointing to it. I decided: I will pray this when I get to Assisi—and maybe even right now.

> Most high,
> glorious God,
> enlighten the darkness of my heart
> and give me, Lord,
> correct faith,
> firm hope,
> perfect charity,
> wisdom and perception,
> that I may do
> what is truly your most holy will.

What is God's will? How would Francis answer? "Kneel with me, and pray these words. And not just once, but over and over, today, and later today, and tomorrow, and the next day." The persistence of Francis's quest for God's will is striking. Like the visitor Jesus told us about, banging on the door at midnight, so relentless he would not stop until the friend inside got up to give him some bread (Luke 11:8), Francis prayed this prayer during an extended period when he wrestled with God, when he struggled to discern God's will for him.

Notice the words *extended period.* Francis prayed this prayer many times, every day, for weeks and then months, for nearly two years—and probably habitually throughout his life. Kneeling beside me, Francis reminds me that God's will isn't something you can just dial up and hear right now; you can't Google it. Nothing worth knowing is so swift, so easy, so cheap. To know the unspeakably rich treasure, you have to look, look again, ask, inquire again, dig, stumble, grow weary, find your legs again, press energetically, fail and fail again, but you continue to strive, restlessly seeking. You knock late into the night and all the next day too. When Francis walked, he would always stop to say his prayers; if he was riding on horseback, he would halt and get down to say his prayers. [1]

The delight is in the quest. The joy is the relationship won by saying to God, "You matter enough, this is important enough, I will not be denied." How lovely were the words Thomas of Celano used to describe this gallant period of Francis's life, and the consistent virtue of all of his existence: "He prayed with all his heart that the eternal and true God guide his way and teach him to do His will. He endured great suffering in his soul, and he was not able to rest until he accomplished in action what he had conceived in his heart."[2]

WHERE DOES PRAYER HAPPEN?

If Francis can teach us about the will of God, we might consider *where* he prayed what he prayed: not just anywhere, but in a church, the small stone chapel called San Damiano, crumbling, unimpressive, but yet a sacred space. Francis took time to get himself bodily to such a place, to invest time in the precincts where the Lord's Supper was blessed and served, where the Word was read and proclaimed, where baptisms and penance and even last rites were performed. What is God's will? Francis says, *Kneel with me, but kneel in a church.* "The LORD is in his holy temple; let all the earth keep silence before him" (Habakkuk 2:20 RSV).

And what was the focal point in this church? A large wooden cross, Romanesque in style, painted a few decades before Francis was born, adorned with complex iconography, featuring small figures of Mary the mother of Jesus, Mary Magdalene, soldiers, onlookers, angels, and even saints like St. Michael, John the Baptist, St. Paul. Hovering above them all is the hand of God the Father, protruding downward out of heaven, in a gesture of blessing.

But dominating the cross, at the heart of it all, is Jesus. We see his body pierced with nails, his head crowned with thorns, the soldier's lance in his side, little streams of blood seeming to squirt from his body. Yet this Jesus seems strong, placid, almost luminescent, his eyes angled so very slightly upward, not fierce but shedding love.

Centuries ago church authorities moved this cross to a more trafficked location in the heart of the city, the beautiful church called Santa Chiara, only about a five-minute walk from my hotel. I decided that a visit to this church, and praying before the cross Francis prayed before, would be a good way to start my day—and might not be a bad way to start any day.

After breakfast, I gathered my things to walk straight to Santa Chiara. *Should I carry the Straub book with me so I can pray the prayer on page 467?* More than six hundred pages in length, it's heavy . . . *I'll just write it down*—which I did, although unnecessarily. How had I missed this on my previous visit? Right outside my hotel, in every shop window, and at the entrance to every church in Assisi, there were little cards with Francis's prayer printed on them. I bought a few, planning to stick them in letters to friends, and to have a handful back home I could give to people who were trying to divine where the water might be.

Then I went in the church. The cross is not visible in the nave, but hangs in a small chapel to the right, the Oratorio del Crocifisso. This crucifix isn't a photo opportunity. The sanctity of the room tugs you down onto your knees. I knelt. Was Francis there? I bowed my head, then gazed up at the face of Jesus, took it all in for a long time, then retrieved the prayer I'd copied, and began to speak to Jesus, silently at first, then in a murmured whisper, and finally, when I noticed no one else was in the room but me, right out loud.

> Most high,
> glorious God,
> enlighten the darkness of my heart
> and give me, Lord,
> correct faith,
> firm hope,
> perfect charity,
> wisdom and perception,
> that I may do
> what is truly your most holy will.

I was—moved? An understatement. I felt the way I imagined that paralyzed man felt when his four friends lowered him through the roof and he found himself face-to-face with Jesus.

I remembered that, after praying this prayer over and over in front of this Jesus, Francis heard Jesus say something from the cross. I found myself wishing Jesus would speak, half believing he might at any moment. I worried that perhaps he just did, but I was too thick in the soul to grasp it. Since that visit, I have kept the little cards with this prayer in my top desk drawer at the office, in my sock drawer at home, and in the little junk compartment that sits under my right elbow when I drive. Has Jesus talked back? Maybe. But my interest in God's will has matured a little, and now and then I find myself thinking—and acting—differently.

I wonder what Francis would say if we gave him a blackboard and chalk and asked him to unpack the prayer. What did his mind gravitate toward when he uttered each phrase, each word?

MOST HIGH, GLORIOUS GOD

Prayer begins with God, not me. Francis knew the height, the grandeur, the sheer massiveness of God, even though his scientific grasp of the universe was paltry. He climbed steep paths to get up higher to pray. He slept out under the stars, and did so when there was virtually no ambient light, no artificial halogens. So as he lay on his back, drifting off, he could see what we can no longer see: a dense array of pinpoints of light, a flurry of meteors streaking, the deep darkness that is not dark to God at all. He would have known the psalm by heart:

> O LORD, our Lord,
>> how majestic is thy name in all the earth!
> Thou whose glory above the heavens is chanted. . . .
> When I look at thy heavens, the work of thy fingers,
>> the moon and the stars which thou hast established;
> what is man that thou art mindful of him,

and the son of man that thou dost care for him?
Yet thou hast made him little less than God,
    and dost crown him with glory and honor.
(Psalm 8:1-8 RSV)

Later we will explore the exuberant delight Francis took in the works of God's fingers.

But when Francis asked, "What is man . . . and the son of man?" he would have thought, not of himself, so small against the canopy of space and the openness of the fields, but of Jesus. What Francis understood about Jesus is that the Most High, Glorious God was not content to hover so high, to remain aloof. That Most High, Glorious God exhibited his glory by coming down, in the humble form of a man, Jesus—and so the height of God is measured by the smallness of Christ come down in the infant Jesus. The prayer for God's will is, like some zoom lens, focused down on something small, tender, alive. God came down from his Most Highness because God loved, God loves—and so God's will is always about love, bending down, humble, serving.

Yet sometimes we pitch God too low, and forget God is Most High. We whittle God down to a size we prefer, a God who exists only to serve me. When Francis prayed this prayer, he was chronically ill. When we are ill, we think it must be God's will for us to feel better—and so we pray, not asking God for how God wants to use me now, or what God is teaching me now, or what God's larger project might be, but merely to be cured . . . understandably! But Francis believed his extended illness broke his stubbornness, humbled him, and opened him up to God in a way he had resisted when he was healthy and virile, with youthful invincibility. When we are agile and energetic, we do not always seek God's will, or we reduce God to a force that should give us a boost along our way. But God is higher than a little boost to my independent life, although I may never glimpse the height of God until I am lying on my back.

God is high. God is more mind-boggling than the scope of stars in the Milky Way. And that God became small and bends down to listen when we begin our prayer with "Most high, glorious

God." Out in the dark, the one who looks up into the darkness really wants just one thing.

ENLIGHTEN THE DARKNESS OF MY HEART

There is darkness out there and in me. Even the most holy, even those intimate with God, have to admit that "we see through a glass, darkly" (1 Corinthians 13:12 KJV). My heart is divided, muddled, and compromised. I have let ugly blockages accumulate; they cast long shadows across my soul. I cannot see where to go or even how to go. I need light.

We may think we are fairly bright, and that we know many things. But only when I look closely and realize my heart is dark, that I cannot see where to go, or how to go, do I open myself to the light of God's will. My brokenness is where I begin. "There is a crack in everything. That's how the light gets in" (Leonard Cohen).

How much light am I seeking? How much do I really need? When I seek God's will, sometimes I foolishly want a brightly illuminated map, with lots of flashing lights, a brilliant clarity, the entire way charted without the slightest uncertainty. But the light God gives is what Francis would have used walking around in the dark of Umbria, when there were no streetlights: a candle, maybe a small torch. How far can you see with a candle? Not far at all.

But perhaps just far enough. Even a flickering candle banishes the darkness, or banishes just enough of the darkness that I can take a step or two, and then I can see a bit farther and take another step or two. I avoid crashing into trees and rocks, I see just far enough, I keep going, I keep looking. God's will is like that. O *God, enlighten the darkness of my heart.* I am not asking for the gleaming brilliance of noon. Just give me sufficient light to take a step or two, then show me what you want to show me next.

AND GIVE ME CORRECT FAITH

What is faith? And what did Francis mean by "correct" faith? Can there be a false faith? When I was in college, without the foggiest interest in God or any kind of spirituality, I took a phi-losophy course on existentialism. The professor assigned me a paper topic: Paul Tillich. I'd never heard of him, but I started researching and discovered him to be a German theologian who came to the United States and taught in Chicago.

The first Tillich book I found in the library was *The Dynamics of Faith.* I'd always thought faith was something you either had or you didn't, and having it might be a good thing and lacking it might be bad, at least to people more interested in religion than I was. But Tillich suggested that we all have faith in something. Faith is what we trust, what we invest ourselves in: faith is my "ultimate concern." And that ultimate concern can be directed to what is false, to what cannot deliver, to what will only delude me and leave me desolate.

Give me a correct faith. Having faith might be dangerous if that faith isn't true, if it isn't passionately committed to what really is God. And is this faith something I conjure up inside myself? No, faith—if Francis is right—is a gift. *Give me correct faith.* On my own I may have no faith, or I may get duped into fawning after all kinds of bogus idols. Again, remember where Francis is pray-ing: in a church, and in front of Jesus. Faith can drift into confu-sion without the loving correction of the Church, its Scriptures, and its Lord. I will discover God's will only when I ask for it as a gift, and when I expect God's will as a by-product of a correct faith, as I have cultivated a relationship with the true God and his Son, Jesus, in the place God has willed for him to be known and for God's will to be revealed.

But we are not alone pursuing God's will *via* a correct faith with Jesus in the Church. The painted cross with which Francis was obsessed depicted disciples, angels, saints, and a holy com-pany of others who also wanted to know God's will. We learn God's will when we let ourselves be swept up in the tide of their prayers, their living out of God's will.

God wills that we relish and benefit from the communion of the saints, God's friends who have asked after God, heard God, failed God, kept seeking God, served God, and now have been ushered into God's presence. They want to help us. They can help us. We rely on God's friends, our brothers and sisters who are veterans of the faith, to inspire and teach us. We cannot see them, but Francis knew that a correct faith always involves hope, "the evidence of things not seen" (Hebrews 11:1 KJV).

FIRM HOPE

Hope is the most stellar of the virtues, and the most distinctively Christian virtue. Hope isn't a sunny optimism that everything will be better tomorrow—although Francis seems to have been born with a sunny, optimistic personality. Hope is a long-term belief in God's ultimate future, which can weather the storm if things get worse tomorrow. Francis endured the worst, and even sought suffering in pursuit of God's will, in unbounded certainty of God's good future.

Hope doesn't depend on you and me getting our act together—although Francis and his friends labored hard to do better each day. Hope depends not on us, but on God, and Francis was buoyed by an unsinkable hope in God, unshakably confident that God would do good, that God would bring everything to its good end, that the future rests securely in God's hands.

If hope is our trust in God's ultimate future, then we can live boldly today. We don't measure our efforts by productivity or the lack thereof; we can do good whether it stands a chance of succeeding or not; we can understand today's small effort as part of God's larger project. Hope liberates us from all calculation; we can live with abandon for God, for those with hope fear nothing. Those with hope can love.

PERFECT CHARITY

For us, the word *charity* denotes something like giving spare change to the needy. But *charity* derives from a Greek word meaning love, grace, free mercy. Francis prayed for love, and he loved with a resplendent passion. God's will is about love. God's will isn't abstract speculation; God's will is that I love, that I am loved, that God loves—and that love is real, practical, sacrificial, tangible, active, lasting.

Could it be that my failure to love is a very dark hole I've fallen into that keeps me from walking around in the daylight of God's will? Or have I trivialized love, reducing it to warm, fuzzy feelings about people I enjoy, or who seem to exist to indulge my desires? Francis's story revolves around what he learned from various encounters with different kinds of people—a knight, a pauper, a noble, friends, his parents—and gradually he pieced together the parts of his life and God's way in the world. Pierre Brunette wrote a book on the *conversions* (plural!) of Francis,[3] and each dramatic moment in that series of conversions happened when Francis came face-to-face with somebody and tried to love them.

The cornerstone meeting came with a leper. Francis admitted that he, like all medieval people, was nauseated at the very sight of lepers, those outcasts suffering from horrific skin maladies, banished from society, thought to be lethally contagious. But as Francis bore witness, "The Lord himself led me among them and I showed mercy to them. And when I left them, what had seemed bitter to me was turned into sweetness of soul and body."[4] He kissed a leper, then another, then another. Much of his life was given to caring for lepers, and it was in his love for the "other," for the one from whom he might have recoiled, that he discovered God's will.

Not merely that it was God's will to love the unlovable! We live out of sync with God, crammed with biases, curved in on ourselves, as if wearing blinders that block us from Jesus—and we can never know God's will until we find the leper and love the leper, discovering in ourselves what is unlovely, and yet also the fact that we too are loved. Then (and only then) we're in the vicinity of hearing and beginning to do God's will.

God's will requires that love called forgiveness. God's will, love, catapults me into situations where I am not the center of the universe. I love, and when I love, I am very close to God's will. If I do not love, and to the degree that I fail to love, I tumble away from God's will.

Such love is hard. So why did Francis then add the adjective *perfect?* My love isn't perfect. But then, neither was Francis's—although his love was astonishing, exemplary, as perfect as we might dream possible. But *perfect* doesn't have to mean flawless, never veering, with crystal, pristine purity. Using Robert's Rules of Order, we *perfect* a motion, which means we try something, and then together we improve upon it. Perfect love tries, improves, refines, and never sinks into complacency.

After all, love enjoys its own peculiar perfection. Try telling a young lover that his devotion to the beloved is less than perfect. We might chuckle at his silliness or immaturity, but in his heart he loves totally, zealously, and will not sleep until he is able to do some little thing the beloved asks. Francis had this kind of love for Jesus.

Maybe perfect love is what Jean Vanier, after a lifetime of serving persons with severe disabilities, spoke of so eloquently:

> To love someone is not first of all to do things for them, but to reveal to them their beauty and value, to say to them through our attitude, "You are beautiful. You are important. I trust you. You can trust yourself." We all know well that we can do things for others and in the process crush them, making them feel that they are incapable of doing things by themselves. To love someone is to reveal to them their capacities for life, the light that is shining in them.[5]

Francis saw beauty in everyone, he crushed no one, he revealed capacity in each person—and that was the fulfillment of God's will.

WISDOM AND PERCEPTION

Was Francis smart? Perhaps, and in chapter 5 we will examine how educated he might have been. But was he wise? Exceedingly so. We may be smart. We see people with dazzling IQs, a knack for turning a buck, or terrific ability at playing the piano or fixing broken things. But where is wisdom?

Wisdom can be had by someone with a low IQ, or someone who lives out in the country and whittles on a porch. Brain brilliance might actually block wisdom; titans of success might be tempted to brush off wisdom as trivial. Ralph Waldo Emerson praised Harvard for having "all the branches of knowledge," only to have Henry David Thoreau retort, "Yes, but none of the roots."[6] Wisdom is deep underground, not just lying around on the surface.

We've made progress technologically since Francis's day; but wasn't Thoreau right when he called most modern inventions "improved means to an unimproved end"?[7] Wisdom thinks about the end, the purpose of life. Wisdom can step out of the moment to understand broader implications. Wisdom is patient, centered, not easily thrown off balance, a kind of serenity. Francis consistently acted as if centered by an inner gyroscope, which is why people witnessed a burst of God's glory in him.

Wisdom is born out of the cauldron of experience: hard times, grief, and sacrifice. You can't just pick up wisdom suddenly, the way you crack open a fortune cookie. You live it, wait on it, test it, let it seep from the good earth through the soles of your feet; you begin to notice you are becoming one with God, who is Wisdom. Francis listened to his life, he paid intense attention to the lives of others, and he could perceive God in it all.

Wisdom is perception—seeing life, the world, and other people from God's perspective. Constant prayer installed this divine vision in Francis's soul. Assuming God's vantage point, Francis saw beneath the surface of things and took the long view, his eye cocked, looking about for not merely what to think but, most important, what to do.

THAT I MAY DO WHAT IS TRULY YOUR MOST HOLY WILL

We typically think it is important to know God's will, to understand God's will, to make sense of God's will, to question God's will. For Francis everything was much simpler. His prayer was not to fiddle around mentally or intellectually with God's will. His passion was, simply, to *do* God's will.

God's will is something we do. We are urged to be "doers of the word, and not hearers only" (James 1:22 KJV). God's will is that we do something. God's desire is that you get in motion, that you act, reach, touch, walk, embrace, lift. For Francis, God's will wasn't a self-absorbed rumination about himself: God's will was about somebody else, a leper, a pauper, a pope, a friend, a stranger. God's will isn't speculative, something to be endlessly debated, forever deferring changes in the pattern of our real lives.

When I first read Nicholas Lash's insightful essay "Performing the Scriptures," I penciled Francis's name in the margin in large letters.[8] Lash wisely reminds us that the Bible is like a script that exists for one reason only: it is to be performed, not merely looked at or studied. We perform the scripture with our words, our deeds, and all of our living and dying in actions that are deliberately in sync with the words, deeds, life, and death of Jesus. We speak of the Holy Bible, but the people who perform it are to be holy.

We may be tempted to counter and say something theologically shrewd, such as, "Aren't we saved by grace, not our deeds?" Indeed. Francis was overwhelmingly grasped by the grace of God as much as or more than any human being about whom we have a witness. It was this extravagance of God's mercy and free largesse that drove Francis to do, to act, to seek relentlessly what God wanted him to do. We are going to do something today, tonight, tomorrow, so why not be determined to make it God's will? And so Francis prayed the prayer we've been exploring and also another one he commended to his friends:

> Almighty, eternal, just and merciful God,
> grant to us miserable ones the grace to do for you
> what we know you want us to do.
> Give us always to desire what pleases you.
> Inwardly cleansed, interiorly illumined
> and enflamed with the fire of the Holy Spirit,
> may we be able to follow in the footprints
> of your beloved Son, our Lord Jesus Christ.[9]

Sometimes Christians speculate about God's will, and many are fond of the idea of the distinction between what God causes and what God merely permits. I wonder what Francis would think? As I have explored the lives of the great saints of history, my sense is that they perceived their lives to be so firmly hinged to God that nothing was conceivable apart from God. The door can open or close, it can creak ajar or slam shut, the light can be streaming through or blocked out—but the door is inseparable from God. So Francis could thank God for little delights and also for pains and struggles. Francis suffered much, but to our knowledge he never asked, *Why?* He embraced whatever he faced; he learned, letting his soul be refined, purified, retooled for further action.

He had plenty of work to do. When Francis prayed before that crucifix, Jesus spoke. But what did Jesus say? "Francis, rebuild my church, for as you can see it is falling into ruin." As we pray for God's will today, could it be that Jesus is again asking us to rebuild the Church? It is falling into ruin, isn't it? Before we explore what it means to rebuild Jesus' Church, we need to take an essential detour and ask Francis about the agonizing cost of doing God's will and the way it ripped his own family apart.

CHAPTER 2
THE VALUE OF POSSESSIONS

I walked with my group of teenage pilgrims to the Piazza del Vescovado in Assisi, and told them that on this very spot Francis renounced all his worldly goods, shedding the very clothes off his back and handing them back to his father. If you ask people about Francis, most associate him with birdbaths; those who know more can quickly tell you that he's the saint (or lunatic) who gave away all his possessions. What was that about?

Farther up the hill in a nearby church, I showed them two precious relics from Francis's life: a gown, and locks of hair. Not *his* locks of hair. His gown, but the locks of hair belonged to the teenage girl who wove the gown: Clare Offreduccio. She had heard Francis preach when she was a young girl; her family's home was snuggled next to the cathedral, San Rufino, where he dazzled the crowds—and her—with his words.

Once she was of age, her parents arranged an advantageous marriage for her (but really for themselves, a ploy to use her to expand their power and property). But what was God's will for her? She was so moved by the vision of Francis that on Palm Sunday of the year 1212, she cast off her possessions and had her hair cut in a symbolic gesture of renunciation of the world. After a few days, her sister did the same. So she, her sister, and other women became followers of Francis, finding their way to San Damiano, where Francis had heard Jesus speak from the cross.

Controversy erupted: it was one thing for men to have nothing and go traipsing about the countryside. But women? They must have possessions as security; if they will not marry, dowries should be donated to abbeys for their endowments—or so they thought in the Middle Ages. But Clare would not be deterred from doing as Francis did, or rather doing as Christ did. She called it "the privilege of poverty,"[1] and the order of women she founded took to heart Jesus' words: "Blessed are you poor, for yours is the kingdom of God" (Luke 6:20 RSV).

Francis gave everything away. Clare gave everything away. Our group thought about Clare and Francis, and wriggling in some discomfort, we raised the question we'd love to ask Francis:

YOU CAN'T EXPECT US TO GIVE AWAY EVERYTHING?

As far as we can tell, Francis never said, "I gave away all I had to the poor and you must do so as well." His expansive, loving heart was incapable of passing judgment. He declined to expend his energy on firing spiritual critique at others; he never smugly cast stones at others whose piety was not so gargantuan. While the Scriptures spoke to him, and he heard Christ's very personal invitation to him to shed his wealth and become poor, Francis would not insist that Christ demands the same thing of everyone. I am not called to be a carbon copy of Francis, and neither are you. Our calling is to seek the One Francis sought, to listen to the One to whom Francis listened, to do what that One asks of us, just as Francis did.

Now that's a relief. I don't have to do as Francis did: I can keep my stuff! But can I? It's not that Francis was acting out some bizarre, utopian notion about poverty. We could safely ignore the lunacy of an Italian misfit from the thirteenth century. But it wasn't Francis's brainchild. It was Jesus who spoke these words: "Sell everything you have and give to the poor" (Luke 18:22 NIV). As we will see in chapter 5, Francis took the Bible literally and with a stunning naïveté. Utterly uninterested in clever explanations of the Bible, Francis took whatever verse he heard as his to-do list for the day.

With Francis, our clumsy, self-indulgent reading of the Bible is exposed. When we hear Jesus say, "Sell everything you have and give to the poor," we brandish our exegetical finesse. No wooden literalism for us! "Jesus means only that we should be *willing* to sell what we have. And if everybody gave everything away, Western civilization would collapse." The very lead-footed people who often stomp around, declaring that "the Bible is clear!" on some issue or another, suddenly become sprightly ballerinas, tiptoeing around what seems clear enough.

A while back I preached on "sell everything you have and give to the poor," and rehearsed the story of Francis. In response, a parishioner dropped by my office to say, "If I sold everything, I wouldn't be able to support *you*." Another paid a visit and gingerly needled me: "I haven't seen *you* sell all you have to give to the poor"—and I overheard myself dance a little jig; I flew into a plié that sounded spiritual, but was no more than a lame defense of my lifestyle preferences. Rationalizing my comforts, where I live and why I have so much, I forgot Francis's wisdom: "It is easier to get to heaven from a hut than from a palace." [2]

Francis never told other people to sell everything, and I certainly don't have to. But I reflect on the life of Francis and its compelling beauty. I recall that, even though Francis never asked them to, young men in Umbria, one after another, sold all they had and gave it to the poor, just like Clare did. Camels were sailing through the eye of the needle at such a pace that the elders of Assisi, many of whose sons and daughters were gallivanting off after Francis (or after Jesus in the company of Francis), quarantined their children, thinking some contagion was on the loose. There was something compelling, something liberating, something alluring about this radical divestment. Apparently it took one person to set the stage, and others were thus granted permission to abandon things and travel light in pursuit of Christ.

WHY LESS IS MORE

What is gained by losing everything? What is the profit in owning nothing? There is the very simple satisfaction of proximity to Jesus, who himself was poor and exhibited not the slightest interest in ownership, earning, accumulating, investing, profiting. There is the joy of simply doing what Jesus said; any life spent with the Bible's admonitions as your marching orders is not a wasted life. There is the curious pleasure of stepping out from the dull conformity of what everybody else is doing and just being a bit strange. Didn't Mother used to say, "If everyone were jumping off a cliff, would you jump too?"

But there is more. How do we define ourselves? How do we measure our worth? I know adults who seem determined to master the children's game of "whoever owns the most toys at the end of the game wins." I get a raise and strut in proud achievement. We fawn after the multimillionaire we happen to encounter. I fret over whether my retirement portfolio is sufficient. The stock market tumbles and heads hang low. Somebody puts a dent in the new car, and temperatures rise. Media moguls on Madison Avenue laugh all the way to the bank, correctly surmising that nobody will pay attention to "thou shalt not covet."

Even in the realm of Church, we have brilliant insights about almost everything except how to think theologically about money. Francis might be able to help, as Murray Bodo wisely suggested:

> The call of Francis, coming as it did at the emergence of a moneyed middle class, was a divine antidote to the disease which would infect society and the individual from then on. One's personal value and self-esteem would by and large be measured in proportion to an ability to make money. Francis saw what money would do to the spirit. Christ alone is the fullness of life, and the compulsive pursuit of money, more than anything else, distracts from what really brings life.[3]

Francis could be my best friend, as I claw my way out of the thicket of money and things into the clear, open air of Christ's love, which cannot be blocked out by the vagaries of economies or accounts. Christ alone really is the fullness of life.

Christ wants to be the fullness of life, not merely out of jealousy, but out of compassion for those of us he made. He knows what makes us tick, what will ruin us, what will free us to thrive. Possessions make outlandish promises to us, but never explain that there is an underside. When Bishop Guido came to Francis to plead with him to hang on to at least a few possessions in order to pursue his work more effectively, Francis replied, "If we had possessions, we would need arms for our protection. For disputes and lawsuits usually arise out of them, and, because of this, love of God and neighbor are greatly impeded. Therefore, we do not want to possess anything in this world."[4]

Possessions promote fear. Thomas of Celano wrote that since Francis and his friends "had nothing, they loved nothing, so they feared losing nothing."[5] Or as Henri d'Avranches phrased it poetically:

> For there is a freedom in poverty
> That makes her the seat of frugality; she is the untroubled rest
> Where virtues lie. She does not sink under weighty worries,
> Nor fear the hand of the thief, nor does she hunt for vanities.[6]

Possessions require security systems, locks, insurance policies, protective coverings. I know a woman who bought a beautiful couch and wanted to preserve the fabric. So she covered it in a different fabric and hollered if houseguests wandered near the thing. Her absurdity is detectable, though, in all of us, especially in the valuables we hoard. Possessions seduce us, and the tail wags the poor dog. Wasn't Francis right in thinking that money is the devil's instrument, the "sacrament of evil"?[7]

WHAT IS THE TRUE VALUE OF POSSESSIONS?

Possessions require arms and time and energy. Not that they lack value! But we subvert their true value by clinging to them, in the same way we ruin relationships with people if we grasp them tightly instead of letting them bloom and flourish freely. Saint Bonaventure described Francis's extraordinary ability to receive gifts: "Whenever anything was given him for his bodily needs, he would always ask the giver for permission to give it away if he should meet one in greater need than himself. He would spare nothing whatever, neither cloak nor tunic nor book, not even vestments or altar cloths, giving everything to the indigent."[8]

Things exist to be given away. Their deepest value, their inherent beauty, is never noticed until they are unwrapped by someone to whom we give them. Our giving is so measured, downright stingy at times, calculating, always balanced against what we think we need later, shrunk by our sense of scarcity. But just as "every good gift . . . is from above, and cometh down from the Father of lights" (James 1:17 KJV), every good thing becomes infinitely more valuable when it is given away. The joy isn't in possessing, but in giving.

No one illustrated this more delightfully than Juniper, one of Francis's friends, who was downright profligate in his exuberance to give:

> So serious was Juniper about imitating Christ that he would give away the very clothes off his back. After several embarrassing episodes, Juniper's superior ordered him not to give his tunic, or any part of it, to a beggar. But soon Juniper was approached by a pauper asking for alms. He replied, "I have nothing to give, except this tunic, and I cannot give it to you due to my vow of obedience. However, if you steal it from me, I will not stop you." Left naked, Juniper returned to the other friars and told them he had been robbed. His compassion became so great that he gave away, not only his own things, but the books, altar linens, and capes belonging to other friars. When the poor came to brother Juniper, the other friars would hide their belongings so he could not find them.[9]

When those church members came by to peck away at my sermon on "sell everything you have and give to the poor," I wish I hadn't gotten flustered but had thought of a wise rejoinder like this: why is it that when we foxily conclude Jesus doesn't mean I have to sell all I have and give it to the poor, therefore, I can go and do whatever I want with my money and things? Did the Gospels include this story so we could ignore it and tell God to mind God's own business? Isn't it in there for some very personal reason that affects me?

Then I've thought of this: if today you sold everything you possessed and gave it to the poor, you would indeed take a huge economic hit. But you would survive. You'd collect your next paycheck. You might inherit something when your parents die. Social security would kick in. You would make it.

But even if you don't sell everything, you could sell more. You could give more. You could take a few chances. You could risk something huge for God. You could give God what really costs you something instead of what costs you nothing. You could reach out to the poor, not with those leftover clothes or canned goods you no longer find desirable, but with something you really like. Maybe you could loosen your grip on things a little. You never know who might admire you for it. In Marilynne Robinson's novel *Gilead*, the narrator speaks of "holy poverty," recalling that "my grandfather never kept anything that was worth giving away." [10]

THE MEANING OF CLOTHES

If we were to inventory our "stuff" and try to assess its monetary value but then also the hidden psychological values buried underneath all of it, and if we could dare to measure the degree to which stuff weighs us down, and what it might feel like to travel lighter, we could begin with clothing. "Clothes make the man." I remember in college, when my attire was typically blue jean shorts, badly frayed, and an old T-shirt that should have been in the laundry or else finding its place as an old rag to use to change the oil, my father would upbraid me for dressing so dreadfully. "Clothes mean nothing to me," I insisted. But the guys I hung around with wore blue jean shorts, badly frayed, old

T-shirts—and come to think of it, all our fathers dressed like one another just as mindlessly, even if more elegantly.

Consider the story of Joseph (Genesis 37–50). His father, Jacob, gave him a "coat of many colors," while his older brothers, clearly not the favorites, wore drab garments. Some scholars believe the better translation would be that Joseph's coat was "long-sleeved," not "multicolored."[11] The social significance is evident: the brothers wore short sleeves, so they could work in the heat of the day. Long sleeves were for lounging in the house; long sleeves would get caught in the brambles out in the field. No wonder they hated Joseph so fiercely. So they sold him as a slave, bloodied the long-sleeved (or multicolored) coat, and shattered their father's heart with the very garment he had given as a sign of his deepest affection.

But Joseph didn't wear the garb of a slave for long. He rose to a position of prominence in Potiphar's house—only to have Potiphar's wife seduce him with her wiles. Too holy to indulge, he scrambled out of her room, but she grabbed his robe, leaving him naked. Now he found himself dressed as a prisoner. Walter Brueggemann made a trenchant observation: "The clothes do not make this man."[12]

But clothes do matter. When we dress each day, or when we shop to compile the wardrobe from which we make that selection, we make a very legible statement to people out there about who we are and where we locate ourselves. Grunge is in the eye of the beholder, isn't it? And fashion isn't some absolute out there; fashion is community. My daughter dressed iconoclastically, dubbing herself a retro hippie. But she was declaring herself by avoiding the chic and donning what felt countercultural—and was joined by her hippie friends. Dress is all about community; clothing is a decision about with whom I will rank myself; my attire is the uniform of the company I keep.

I took my group of teenagers through the magnificent basilica featuring the frescoes narrating Francis's life. Fabric, brilliantly colored cloth, figures prominently in virtually every memorable vignette. In one fresco we viewed, a gallant admirer of the young and very hip Francis spread out his cape (a gesture reminiscent to us of Sir Walter Raleigh and the queen) so Francis wouldn't muddy his feet. Walking a few feet farther into the basilica, we saw another fresco, with a peasant asking Francis for a bolt of fabric. Francis refused, but later realized that if a wealthy man had asked, he would have given it.

Francis disrobed and gave his exotic clothing back to his father. Francis "changed clothes." He changed not just from one shirt to another. He trashed an entire fashion line, a way of life, a convention where his clothing located him in the upper echelon of society, and he picked up an old sack, made it into a robe, gave away his jewel-studded leather belt, and bound himself with an old piece of rope.

But why? Francis was shedding his past. We might recall the way the early Christians came to be baptized: they took off their old, dirty work clothes, descended into the water, and then as they emerged they were wrapped in new, white robes. The symbolism of new life was articulated beautifully by Paul: "Put on then, as God's chosen ones, holy and beloved, compassion, kindness, lowliness, meekness, and patience . . . [and] put on love" (Colossians 3:12, 14 RSV).

Literal reader of the Bible that he was, Francis knew Jesus did not wear the grandest fashions; he did not mimic the Romans with their exotic or militaristic attire. He wore what the plainest peasants wore—and Francis wanted to be like Jesus. I think Francis would also say that clothing can be just plain dishonest. We pretend to be somebody we aren't. To dress like a penniless beggar, to wear the garments of the poor is to speak truthfully on the outside about who we are on the inside. Luther was right: "We are beggars, and that is all." G. K. Chesterton put it eloquently:

> His argument was this: that the dedicated man might go anywhere among any kind of men, even the worst kind of men, so long as there was nothing by which they could hold him. The friar was freer than the ordinary man. There was nothing the world could hold them by. A man had to be thin to pass through the bars and out of the cage; he had to travel light to travel fast and far. You could not threaten to starve a man who

was ever striving to fast. You could not ruin him and reduce him to beggary, for he was already a beggar.[13]

Do you sense the freedom in an honest poverty? Murray Bodo was on target: "Francis strikes at the heart of the hypocrisy of his world, where reputation is more important than goodness and truth. . . . In choosing 'failure' from the outset, Francis frees himself from the enormous burden of the opinion of others."[14]

CHANGING CLOTHES WITH THE POOR

Francis also knew that his vocation was to connect with the poor. You can't build many bridges to the poor if you don't want to get your French fashions tangled in the briars or muddied in a pigsty. Mother Teresa, we might forget, began her adult life as a teacher to affluent Bengali girls in Calcutta. But in 1946, on the train to Darjeeling, she heard a voice calling her to reach out to the poorest of the poor. She did not visit them by day and return to the security of her school by night. She changed clothes literally and figuratively.

At first, she had no helpers, no money, no shelter, no security. With a small bag, she walked into the slums, unsure where to go. Like the poor, she had to search on foot for a roof over her head. She began to understand the exhaustion of the poor, how food is scarce, how medicine is inaccessible. She rented a little hut for five rupees a month and invited children to her makeshift school. Most of her time was spent in the work of bathing, carrying, and feeding.

Other young women followed her into the barrios; and just as Francis's friends divested themselves of wealth to become his friars, most of these women found themselves in a rapid descent to the nether layers of India's caste system. Once a wealthy Hindu woman came, offering aid. During the conversation, she admitted how much she loved beautiful saris; in fact, she spent 800 rupees each month on a new sari. Mother Teresa, whose distinctive white cotton sari with a blue stripe cost 8 rupees, thought this the place to begin. "Next time, when you go to buy a sari, instead of buying a sari for 800 rupees, you buy a sari worth 500 rupees and with the remaining 300 you buy saris for the poor people." More than the reallocation of money was at stake; the elegance of a sari was a symbol of a woman's status, her notch in the caste system. But the woman did it. The next month she paid 400 rupees for her own sari, then 300 the next month, until she was down to just 100 rupees for herself, giving the rest away. Mother Teresa urged her, "Please do not go below 100!" The woman reported that her life was transformed, that she received far more than she ever gave.[15]

So, as we continue to converse with Francis, what exactly am I going to wear tomorrow? How heavy is my wardrobe nowadays? One small success in my friendship with Francis and fledgling attempts to get closer to Jesus occurred in Lithuania. My daughter and I had gone to visit a small Methodist congregation in Siauliai. Beautiful Christians in an economically depressed zone behind what used to be the Iron Curtain displayed Francis-like hospitality as we toured, prayed, preached, and built lasting friendships. My daughter Sarah and I were especially pleased to visit Lithuania's holiest shrine, the "hill of crosses," and then to discover an adjacent monastery with stained glass devoted to the life of Francis.

The day came to fly home, and I was packing. I was feeling a bit grumpy, weary after weeks of travel, anticipating the drudgery of long waits, checking and then probably losing bags, the line through customs getting bogged down, my herniated disk inflamed. Then the shadow of St. Francis crept across my vantage point, and I had this thought: *Why cram these clothes into this suitcase? Why don't I just leave them here? I'll sail right through customs, and my back won't ache from hauling the luggage.*

So I started to unpack. Pants, another pair of pants, a shirt, a tie, a jacket, another shirt. This was getting to be fun, thinking of the young men I'd met who would feel cooler in these American clothes than I'd ever felt in them. But then there was a sweater—the sweater my wife had just given me for Christmas, beautiful, carefully chosen. *Okay, I'll leave most of my clothes but take this sweater home.*

But then what would Lisa think? Hadn't I married the kind of woman who would be annoyed with me if I left most of my clothes, but thought her sweater was too good to leave behind? So I left that one too. And I can tell you that I have enjoyed all of those clothes, and especially the new Christmas sweater, far more knowing they are being worn by friends in Lithuania than if I had them in my wardrobe here at home. I haven't gone naked one day since then. And I was afforded a small taste of what Francis and Juniper and Mother Teresa's friend understood so well: the joy of giving it all away.

Francis would have made a good hobbit. I wish I knew if J. R. R. Tolkien ever thought about the little man from Assisi when he was writing about the smallish heroes of *The Lord of the Rings*. Hobbits have an intriguing way of celebrating their birthdays. Instead of receiving gifts, hobbits give gifts on their birthdays. My children read up on this, and as my birthday approached, they suggested this would be a fascinating experiment. And so began our custom, stretching over several years now: on my birthday, realizing there frankly isn't anything purchasable that I want or need, I give gifts to my wife and children, never something they have bothered to ask for, just something I want them to have.

There is a curious virtue to giving our stuff away, especially if we don't go to the mall to buy new stuff to give away but actually give our own stuff away. We have less, we travel lighter; we are freer, not so tied down. Life, after all, is a pilgrimage; we are in exile temporarily down here or at least so the saints of old taught us. And we need not be alone. Francis's spendthrift giving was contagios; he had good company in his giving. When I tell friends about the hobbit birthday scheme, or leaving your clothes in another country, many of them—most of them?—decide they will give it a try. And then it's not just me doing something ridiculously delightful; I have good company. We are not alone.

And that's how giving works anyhow. We try to assess why there is poverty and what the solution might be. The only answer is discovering each other's company. Jürgen Moltmann wisely suggested that "the opposite of poverty isn't property. The opposite of both poverty and property is community."[16] Then we are no longer possessed by our possessions. And our newfound poverty, even if it's a partial poverty, a poverty only comparatively more poor than the affluence I thought I enjoyed yesterday, there's a new space, a little more room for God and for the new friend in need God places before me.

But when we discover new friends and find more room for God, there is a cost, one that can be excruciating to bear, as Francis can show us.

CHAPTER 3

THE DILEMMA OF FAMILY

One day, Francis heard God say,

> Francis, everything you have loved carnally and desired to have, you must despise and hate, if you wish to know my will. Because once you begin doing this, what before seemed delightful and sweet will be unbearable and bitter; and what before made you shudder will offer you great sweetness and enormous delight.[1]

Doing God's will thrust Francis into an unbearable and bitter conflict with his own father. When I think of Francis, and the various scenes from his life, I find myself uncertain how to feel about the dramatic moment when Francis's father sued his own son in the public square. Is this a glimpse of titanic faith I should try to emulate? Isn't there a terrible heartbreak when a father and son part ways—and over God? Am I frightened that I will wind up with a fractured relationship with my own children? How do I remember the way I responded to what I thought was God's call for my life, and yet left my father befuddled?

DOES FAITH DIVIDE THE FAMILY?

What is the deal with God and family? For years now we have heard laments over the erosion of the family, and it seems like

God ought to dole out some family medicine, God ought to be the glue to hold the family together. But does it really work that way? Can faith redirect a family? Might faith divide a family? What if I begin to suspect that God is luring me someplace—or has already transported me to someplace—that my parents cannot comprehend? That my spouse recoils from? That would elicit little from my children except a bored shrug?

Leo Tolstoy's first sentence in *Anna Karenina* was this: "Happy families are all alike; each unhappy family is unhappy in its own way." How was Francis's family unhappy? Wouldn't we expect a saint to have grown up in a happy family? Why is it that dysfunction and heartbreak give birth not just to craziness but (more often than we like to admit) to brilliance, creativity, and even sanctity?

Let's travel back in time to the day of the trial. We can imagine the tittering gossip rifling through the city, its citizens turning out to see this soap opera play out in the picturesque Piazza del Vescovado. The drama was captured most memorably in fresco, and in living color we see the story's climax: Francis has returned every worldly possession he has left to his father—and that wasn't much after months of extravagant sharing with the poor! All he had to return to his father were the clothes on his back. Stark naked, Francis stands before his father, but his eyes are fixed upward, where we see a hand framed in blessing extending down from the clouds.

At just this moment, Francis said, "Until now I have called Pietro Bernardone my father. But, because I have proposed to serve God, I return to him the money on account of which he was so upset, and also all the clothing which is his, wanting to say from now on: 'Our Father who are in heaven,' and not 'My father, Pietro di Bernardone.' "[2] The bishop, Guido, is covering Francis's nakedness with his cloak. Partly he wants to shield Francis's shame from onlookers. But the cloak is also symbolic of the Church's blessing and the Church's protection. The nudity might rattle our prudish sensibilities, but the lack of clothing is a fascinating spiritual image: just as Francis (and each one of us) came into the world naked, so we leave it naked. Jesus on the cross was stripped naked when he commended his soul to God his Father.

ISN'T ALL LOVE FLAWED?

How did Francis feel? We don't know. He has made a ringing theological statement, and yet to have the door to his home and his father slammed shut, to bear the horrible brunt of his father's rage against everything that was beautiful and meaningful for Francis, to see the shamed disappointment in his father's eyes, and to inflict carnage on his mother: this climactic moment had to devastate his sensitive soul.

If Francis refused to step on an ant, if he kissed lepers he'd never met before, if he befriended the Muslim sultan, how could he unleash such emotional pain on his mother and father? Was it "telescopic philanthropy"[3]—Dickens's phrase describing how it may be easier to love those at a distance? We have seen such people, and many wind up in the ministry and helping professions: deeply, passionately devoted to the poor, to strangers, to parishioners, but woefully unable to connect with spouse or children at home.

"Francis is the son of Pietro Bernardone, and no decision to call only God his father can change that. The placid son of God is also the volcanic son of Bernardone," Murray Bodo reminds us.[4] Did Francis sleep soundly that night? We do not know. But we may suspect that some dark sword pierced his tender heart. And there was a lifetime of nights and days ahead; shattered relationships are still relationships, and the broken pieces keep wounding you. For years, "whenever his father met him on the street he would curse him."[5]

Or so most of Francis's biographers tell us. But is that the whole truth? One early version of Francis's life frames the conflict differently, telling us that when Pietro saw Francis's plight, he was very sad, "for he loved him dearly."[6] Was Pietro entirely an icy Machiavellian? Didn't he love his son dearly? Perhaps his love was flawed. But then, isn't all love flawed?

And didn't Francis recognize that his love for his father might have been flawed in some way? Sainthood must bear the agonies of failure somewhere. If I could ask Francis a few questions, I would explore the way he remembered his father in his heart. *What did you try to say to him? How did you pray for him?* And what I would most want to know: *Did you ever reconcile, even late in life, perhaps on your father Pietro's deathbed?* We do not know. I worry that this fantasy of reconciliation never happened, that Pietro died without the consolation of his son kissing him good-bye.

But if so, was even that sorrow the end of things? The churches of Assisi have frescoes depicting Francis and a host of friars and sisters and lepers and angels in heaven; for them, life went on beyond the grave. Could it be that, in God's mind-boggling grace, Francis met up with Pietro in heaven? Or might he have descended the steps into purgatory to meet with him there? Wouldn't Francis seize that chance to converse with his father, to listen one more time, to embrace, even to say he was sorry, to receive his father's long-delayed blessing? Nicholas Wolterstorff, reflecting on the death of his son, asked,

> What do I do with my regrets? A friend warned me against this question. Don't rehearse your regrets, he said. But they come to mind unrehearsed. Should I try to stop them? I believe that God forgives me. I do not doubt that. The matter between God and me is closed. But what about the matter between Eric and me? For my regrets remain. What do I do with my God-forgiven regrets? I shall live with them. And I shall allow them to sharpen the vision and intensify the hope for that Great Day coming when we can all throw ourselves into each other's arms and say, "I'm sorry." The God of love will surely grant us such a day. Love needs that.[7]

Didn't God grant Francis and his father such a day?

HOW DID IT ALL UNRAVEL?

We are racing too far into the future. Back to the trial, the tragic split between father and son. How did things come to such an impasse? There had always been a marked distance between Francis and his father. Most fathers in those days were emotionally remote; the home was the mother's domain. Perhaps as an intimation of things to come, Francis was born while Pietro was out of the country on business. According to those legends that strain credulity to make Francis sound like a second Jesus, Francis was born in a stable. But Pietro gave his wife, Pica, everything; it is hard to believe she would leave the comforts of their upstairs home to descend into the vaulted stable beneath—although the little prayer chapel there today, called San Francesco Piccolino, invites you to pray where Francis entered the world among the oxen, sheep, and donkeys. Francis did have a lifelong affinity for such humble creatures.

Pietro Bernardone was an up-and-coming merchant who dealt in exotic French and Flemish fabric. His travels took him to the great marketing fairs in Champagne; growing up with such a father, Francis came to be enamored with French manners, music, and dress. Not only did Pietro's business acumen bring an exotic hipness to Francis's youth; Pietro had also purchased prized plots of land around Assisi, olive groves, fields—resources, an unshakable security for his family, the perfect foil for the kind of saint Francis became. In a way, Francis never could have become Francis were it not for the burgeoning affluence of his father.

While we would probably admire Pietro as a sharp opportunist, climbing the social ladder to join the wealthy elite, Francis's first biographer took a dim view of his father's activities, including his intentions for Francis: "His parents reared him to arrogance in accordance with the vanity of the age. And by long imitating their worthless life and character he himself was made more vain and arrogant." [8]

Francis's parents wanted him to fit in, to live "in accordance with the vanity of the age." Perhaps parents nowadays might beware of contemporary culture and discern the ways faith might put their children at odds with today's "vanities." Don't we mindlessly hope that our children will fit in, be normal, and succeed by the world's standards? Don't we steer them to be properly fashionable, to have the best friends possible, to do everything everyone else is doing?

Spending money extravagantly, even foolishly, was simply being "cool" in their culture (and ours!): this is what those in high society were able and eager to do. Folly was expected from the youth in the upper classes. Could Lawrence Cunningham be right? He wrote, "Francis seems to have been a typical indulged, wealthy, spoiled, and thrill-seeking adolescent who was indulged by a family who could afford to look with a benevolent eye on the peccadilloes of youth."[9] At indulgent thrill-seeking, his parents could wink and chalk it up to "boys will be boys." But becoming a saint? Why is sanctity harder to grasp than the sophomoric party life?

But lumping both parents together is unfair to Francis's mother. Pica (perhaps a nickname? Was she from Picardy in

France?) was portrayed by Henri d'Avranches as "upright, unpretentious and kind,"[10] and by later biographers as a woman of immense faith, drawing comparisons to Elizabeth, the mother of John the Baptist. When his father locked him up in jail, she sneaked to the prison by night and let her son go, much to Pietro's consternation.

It would be interesting to study the lives of heroes of faith and chart how many come from such divided homes. Could it be that the peaceful home marked by spiritual harmony might be too placid to stir a radical faith in children? Patricius was the cold, raging-tempered father of St. Augustine, who overheard his mother Monica's constant prayers: "She strove in every way that you, my God, would be my father rather than he."[11] Were Pica's prayers answered when Francis shunned Pietro and turned to God as Father?

JESUS AND FAILURE

How did Francis's father wind up tossing his son in jail? The story is familiar enough, but we dare not romanticize it. Pietro strutted proudly the day his son marched off to war with Perugia. But after the battle was lost and Francis was captured, was he disappointed in his son's performance? Certainly Francis's bizarre behavior, his wild dreams, his oddball afternoons in trances and prayer would have befuddled Pietro.

Determined to rebuild crumbling churches and to provide succor for the poor, Francis began to sell and then give away bales of exotic cloth—his father's cloth. Unwittingly, unknowingly, Pietro actually assisted in the rebuilding of the Church and in a mission to clothe the poor! But he had no desire to continue and was ferociously angry at his son's insolence. "Striving to bend Francis's will to his own, he badgered him, beat him and bound him." But a hidden good surfaced: "As a result of this Francis became more fit and eager to carry out his holy plan."[12]

Francis did not bolt from his father's house in an instant. In chapter 1 we mentioned Pierre Brunette's notion of the conversions—plural—of Francis: "It took Francis of Assisi some six or seven years to discover the Gospel as a way of life. He experienced many conversions . . . a lengthy inner maturation."[13] Nothing came quickly or easily. Francis made his decisions about following Christ, but then hid for weeks at San Damiano, fearful of his father's rage, unable to face his family's crushing disappointment. The day came when the final act could be postponed no longer. Desperate, embarrassed, unwilling to let himself be a laughingstock or to lose another bolt of cloth and the gold he could sell it for, Pietro took his son to court.

I find myself imagining Pietro sitting at the bar with his affluent, on-the-rise friends, lamenting his son's failure, being sure to add words like "after all I've done for him . . ." Bodo helps us understand Francis's "failure":

> Francis strikes at the heart of the hypocrisy of his world, a world for whom reputation and good name is more important than goodness and truth. . . . In choosing "failure" from the outset, Francis frees himself from the enormous burden of the opinion of others.[14]

Including, sadly, the opinion of family. Parents, for all their powerful emotions and salient dreams for their children, have limited access to the drama transpiring between God and their children. My father harbored a grand vision for me, but could he see what was happening in my soul? Can I see this in my children? Or in my spouse? When do I have wisdom from God for them? And when is my wisdom nothing more than my own narrow preference? And if I have wisdom, how do I share and leave space for them to live into God's call?

The difficulties are many, and Jesus sticks a dagger into the thing and mercilessly twists it by saying,

> "I have come to set a man against his father, and a daughter against her mother, and a daughter-in-law against her mother-in-law; and a man's foes will be those of his own household. He who loves father or mother more than me is not worthy of me; and he who loves son or daughter more than me is not worthy of me." (Matthew 10:35-37 RSV)

And even more harshly:

> "If any one comes to me and does not hate his own father and mother and wife and children and brothers and sisters, yes, and even his own life, he cannot be my disciple." (Luke 14:26 RSV)

Clearly we are light-years from the Jesus invented by modern spiritual leaders, the manufactured Jesus who props up family values or notions such as "the family that prays together stays together." The gospel poses a stark decision, and to say *yes* to the call of God at times (or frequently? or maybe always?) entails a break with family. Many families are not very serious about God. Those that are need to prepare themselves to be shocked by what God might do.

We pray the Lord's Prayer regularly. What does it mean to call God "our Father"? We fret over the gender issue, as we should. But think about Francis. Instead of praying the "our Father" the way the Church has often taught us to pray, to expect that we can "pray with complete confidence, just as children speak to their loving father" (as Luther urged in his *Small Catechism*), we might notice an edge, a hidden connotation: for Francis, to pray to "our Father" took on the nuance of a declaration of allegiance, to the exclusion of other, even admirable, allegiances. "No longer is Pietro my father"; no longer will I sit passively in the prison of family expectations, which are only blocking God's fresh work in me.

IS THERE HOPE FOR FAMILY?

But family need not be feared as pure peril! And even if we suffer the loss of family, because of division and dysfunction, or because of death or physical separation, the benefits of family are not entirely jettisoned. Francis was not anti-family; in fact, his life's most passionate endeavor was the fashioning of a new family. What had Jesus said?

> "Who is my mother, and who are my brothers?" And stretching out his hand toward his disciples, he said, "Here are my

mother and my brothers! For whoever does the will of my Father in heaven is my brother, and sister, and mother." (Matthew 12:48-50 RSV)

Francis did not recruit henchmen or assistants, apprentices or students. He called them "friars," which means "brothers." Under what Francis called "universal fatherhood of God," we find ourselves in a new family whose firstborn is Christ. In a letter to the men and women gravitating into his new family, Francis exclaimed, "We are brothers when we do the will of His Father who is in heaven. . . . O how holy and how loving, gratifying, humbling, peace-giving, sweet, worthy of love, and above all things desirable it is to have such a Brother and such a Son: our Lord Jesus Christ."[15]

With his poetic imagination, Francis extended the family image beyond brothers, with the Father and Son. Visitors to Assisi can see a handwritten letter from Francis to Brother Leo that begins tenderly: "I am speaking, my son, in this way—as a mother would." [16] We would expect a Catholic in the Middle Ages to stick with "father." But Francis slipped into a more gentle, feminine guise. "I am speaking as a mother would"—and perhaps as Francis's own mother did. Worn spots on the parchment letter lead experts to believe Leo kept this letter with him for many years as a precious keepsake. And some who have analyzed the letter feel that Francis's handwriting indicates he was suffering from wounds in his hands as he wrote, but more on that later.

To the young men gathered around him, Francis said, "We are brothers." To the young women, like his beloved friend Clare Offreduccio, he said, "We are brothers and sisters." But the spiritual kinship extended beyond just male and female people. Francis looked at animals, the birds, fish, even ravenous wolves, and called them brother or sister. Trees, rivers, flowers, mountains, the elements of all creation, fire, sun, rain, and the earth were his sisters and brothers.

This vision is compelling, intriguing, even inviting. But most of us still find ourselves living in the thick of some family. I have a wife, and three children not yet on their own. I have a father and a mother, divorced, and a sister, unmarried. I have in-laws whose kids are grown and married, out of the house. I tend to count my closest friends as family; my children call my college friends Tom and Randy "Uncle Tom" and "Uncle Randy." Who is family? How do we live as family and in families? What is best for my family?

From Francis we learn that to paint a churchly veneer over family life accomplishes nothing. Pietro went to church and took Communion; but his worldview was shaped more by the economics of merchant life and the politics of feudal tension than by the Church. Perhaps we could step back and look at our life together and ask about our genuine purpose. Most families are striving to be—what?—happy. But what would happen if a family asked, not "How can we be happy?" or "What can we do to have fun?" but "How can we be faithful?"[17] or "What can we do to serve God today?"

When I took our church's teenagers to Assisi, we spoke of the way Francis touched lepers, the untouchables nobody wanted to be around. I asked our group, "Who are the lepers we avoid but might touch?" Many thoughtful answers ensued, but the most striking came from one young woman, who said, "For me it's my siblings. I am greedy about time, and I make time for friends, for school, for various activities. But do I take time for my younger siblings?" Do our families become the "lepers," the untouchables we need to touch for the sake of Christ?

With whom do we socialize as a family? Look at children's birthday parties, or the people you have over to your house for a picnic or a dinner party. The people most of us hang around with look a lot like us in terms of race, educational background, economic status. But Francis crossed every boundary. What will the family striving to learn from the revolutionary of Assisi do? We might, when it's time for cake and games, deliberately gather children who do not all look alike, whose parents do not hold similar jobs; we might invite someone who lives in another part of town to our home and plan to have dinner with someone of a different culture. We would be sure that the poor are not strangers we view across a chasm but friends whose names and lives we know and are involved in.

Parents always want to "provide" for their children. Pietro was a well-funded provider, yet he failed to provide the one thing needful: space for God, an openness to where God would take his son. Can I provide my children with a faithful life, an exemplary goodness that dares something bold for God, that includes the poor or disenfranchised? Why can't I focus on the one thing that matters: that my children will pray and discern God's call?

Can a marriage be more Franciscan? Francis lived in a way that enabled women, like Clare and her sister and many others, to find their way to serve God. Perhaps a marriage can be riveted to God. Perhaps serving the poor, worshiping, praising, and having an active life of kinship with people and nature would be not merely *on* the agenda; all this would *be* the agenda.

Just to know and talk about the life of Francis can bring new vision, healing, and hope to any family or friendship. In our home, we have a painting of Francis preaching to the birds, we have a statue of Francis in the garden, we have icons of Francis, and we have framed three of his prayers and placed them in the bathroom, in the bedroom, and in the den. Having a saint as a guest in your home can be just another artistic sidebar, or you can think of Francis as a conversation partner, a reminder, someone who is watching you, loving you, encouraging you. He's happy to be part of the family. When the kids were little, we created a little puppet show and staged dramatic moments from the life of Francis.

Vacations can be built around lessons from Francis's life. Instead of going to the beach or a fun resort with your time off, you can go to a hurricane-ravaged zone and engage in relief work together. Or most anywhere you go, you can find a way to remember the poor and step out of the tourist's mentality of conspicuous consumption. The first time I went to Rome, my friend took me to a shelter, and I found myself spooning up soup and then scrubbing a toilet on the day I had expected to be touring an art museum. The beauty was more real and unforgettable.

I have taken two of my daughters to Assisi, and eventually I will take my son. My oldest, Sarah, kept a journal as we walked where Francis walked, sat in the churches where he worshiped, and ate in the streets where he lived. She penned this poem:

you, dear San Francesco
who shunned our earth's possessions—
frozen now in fresco
i trace your life's progression
you, from high society
came down the shielding hill
to bend to holy piety
and to do God's will
your prayers were oh so faithful
you dwelled within God's grace
you hated all things hateful
and longed to see God's face
and so to lasting saintdom
you have finally come
your love, meant for God's kingdom,
came down, and struck me dumb

Francis strikes us dumb when he calls us brothers, sisters, a new family of God. We have a word for this odd family: *the Church*— and we would like to ask Francis a few questions about this curious institution.

CHAPTER 4

THE SMALLNESS OF THE CHURCH

When I moved to a new parish quite a few years ago now, one of the lay leaders suggested we kick off our ministry together by holding a series of neighborhood meetings, focused on the question, "What's wrong with the Church?" He added, "You could probably write a book on that!" No doubt, and it could run long into multiple volumes, thick with all the words printed in a small font. We rightly nixed the idea: too easy a target. Surveying what's wrong with the Church, we don't know whether to blush, groan, or shake our heads. The Church forever teeters on the edge of fluffy triviality, mock caricature, and the outright demonic.

Surely St. Francis, one so holy, so close to Jesus, would have deep insights into the foibles of the Church. We might wish we could hire him to lead a workshop on the matter; he could be a consulting guru, diagnosing all that has gone awry, and what drastic measures must be taken now for the Church to recover or simply to survive.

WHAT'S WRONG WITH THE CHURCH?

While we have no record of Francis entertaining this question, I feel relatively certain I know precisely how he would reply. "What's wrong with the Church?" His startling answer?

"Nothing."

Nothing? Admittedly, Francis was not disposed to faultfinding. But that isn't the whole story. Francis, to our knowledge, never criticized the Church or drew up grand plans for its demolition and reconstruction. He exhibited a warmth and obedient humility in the face of all Church authorities, both the noble and the crass, the holy and the decadent. Francis never for one moment stepped outside the Church or thought of his movement as any kind of alternative to the Church. History has probably never witnessed a more thoroughgoing Church insider.

Not that Christians in Francis's day cowered in fear of Church authority and dared not speak: reform was in the air. Countless movements, like that of the Waldensians, sprang up across Europe, politicking for radical change in a Church that had become corrupt. Other saints who lived near the time of St. Francis launched critical tirades against the opulence of the Church. The grandest bastion of the medieval Church, the cathedral at Cluny, was derided by St. Bernard; scoffing at the monks' vestments, the splendor of the sanctuary's columns, he expostulated,

> I say nothing of the height of your churches, their immoderate length, their superfluous breadth, the costly polishings, the curious carvings and paintings which attract the worshipper's gaze and hinder his attention. . . . At the very sight of these expensive yet marvelous vanities men are more inclined to offer gifts than to pray. . . . How do they keep the Rule who are clad in furs? [1]

Francis knew and exuded the richest appreciation for the Church's treasures. Not the polishings, furs, and vanities but the Church's genuine, humbler, more lasting treasures—such as the Scriptures, of course. Every church is like some ark of the covenant, a manmade box rendered holy because of its contents, the Word of God.

Francis passionately revered the Sacraments. He was baptized in the Church,[2] where promises were made, the Spirit came down, the creed was professed. I recall being in the basilica in

Assisi and witnessing a Baptism; quite a number of times, in the basilica, but also San Damiano and the other churches of Assisi, I have participated in the Lord's Supper. As I tried to follow the Italian, which tantalizingly echoes the Latin that Francis would have heard in worship as a child, there were enough loanwords familiar to me, an English speaker and hearer, to follow along. We are baptized into the Church, to live in the Church.

And to die in the Church. Francis was on a long journey when his health finally failed him. His last expenditure of energy was to get back home to Assisi—but not merely to the city. He wanted to die in the Church, and he did, lingering long enough to breathe his last in his much beloved chapel, Santa Maria degli Angeli. Rumor had it that the bells of a neighboring church, San Stefano, spontaneously rang out in the dark. At first, they buried Francis in San Giorgio, and then they transferred his body to the massive new basilica built in memory of him. Today, the stone crypt housing his body, around which his closest friends were also buried, is a chapel of unmistakable sanctity.

His birth and death were in the Church, and so was all that transpired in between. Francis got himself physically inside some church virtually every day of his forty-four years on earth. The body and blood of our Lord, the reading of the Gospels, the feast days, the priests, the art, the very walls and air: Francis loved everything about the Church and its treasures.

Speaking of its treasures, Francis would have understood better than any of us the marvelous story of St. Lawrence: facing the trauma of persecution in third-century Rome, Lawrence was given three days by the prefect of Rome to round up the treasures of the Church and surrender them to Caesar. At the appointed time, he knocked on the prefect's door and presented him with a throng of people for whom the Church was caring—the poor, those who were blind or lame, lepers, and orphans—proudly announcing, "These are the treasures of the Church." Caring nothing for all that was gilded and golden, Francis magnificently expanded the Church's true treasures.

IS THE BIGGER CHURCH BETTER?

In a way that might strike us as countercultural today, Francis had a heart for the small, broken-down churches to which nobody else was drawn. He found his very self in such a church and discovered Jesus (or was discovered by Jesus) in a ramshackle, crumbling sanctuary we'd bulldoze today. So, for all little churches that feel forgotten or unimportant, too small to attract today's consumer-minded churchgoers, Francis offers comfort and hope: the greatest of saints discovered his call, not in any of the huge cathedrals on which architectural geniuses were putting their finishing touches in those days, but inside San Damiano.

Today many tourists somehow miss this little church, although it is the spiritual birthplace of all that is powerful about Francis. Leaving the Porta Nuova gate, you can walk there pretty easily, although the hike back up the steep incline exhausted me and my daughter one blazing July afternoon. So we sat on a stone bench in the shade and thought through the story together.

San Damiano had been standing for more than a hundred years and was showing signs of its age when Francis stepped inside. Having returned from the war with Perugia, injured, distraught, confused about his identity, flailing to discover his future, Francis walked to this tiny sanctuary each day and prayed—and his words were the prayer we spent time on in the first chapter:

> Most high,
> glorious God,
> enlighten the darkness of my heart
> and give me, Lord,
> correct faith,
> firm hope,
> perfect charity,
> wisdom and perception,
> that I may do
> what is truly your most holy will.

His prayer was focused on that Romanesque cross. Finally Jesus spoke to Francis from that cross. And what did Jesus say?

"Francis, rebuild my church, for as you can see it is falling into ruin."

Francis heard. And then he acted. With no small amount of naïveté, Francis thought Jesus meant for him to rebuild San Damiano—and he did. This is how the rebuilding of the Church—big Church, with a capital C, *the* Church universal— begins: by rebuilding this church, right here, today, the little one. Karl Barth, perhaps the most brilliant theologian of the twentieth century (or any other!), wrote his most stunning work while pastor of a very small church in Safenwil, Switzerland. Snugly within its walls, he realized a grandiose vision for every church:

> I believe that the congregation to which I belong . . . is the one, holy, universal Church. If I do not believe this here, I do not believe it at all. No lack of beauty, no "wrinkles and spots" in this congregation may lead me astray. . . . In faith I attest that the concrete congregation to which I belong and for the life of which I am responsible, is appointed to the task of making in this place, in this form, the one, holy, universal Church visible. [3]

Jesus told Francis, "Rebuild my church." Not "go and be more spiritual than even the Church," not "tear down or circumvent the Church," not "start a parachurch movement that will trumpet the real Christianity," but "rebuild my Church." My Church! Jesus' Church. Not Francis's, not the pope's, not mine, not yours. Dilapidated San Damiano did not appear very promising. But Jesus had said, "Rebuild my church."

So, Francis started, stone by stone, and did so with his own hands. We might not realize the embarrassment this caused: people of his social class simply did not work with their hands, did not lift stones, did not get dirty. But very tenderly, yet with a muscular hopefulness, Francis picked up its fallen stones. Using masonry skills he'd honed in his days with the army as a would-be knight reconstructing the military fortress of Assisi, Francis engaged in a little repair work, envisioning so much that was right with San Damiano. Through most of his adult life, Francis carried a broom so that if he happened upon a church that had gathered dust and cobwebs, he could clean the place up a bit.

Now that's different from our modern era, when people flock in droves to the big, slick churches with flawlessly manicured yards and the latest technological gadgets. Francis would shudder. His heart soared over little San Damiano. "It's just a building!" we may wish to say. But W. H. Vanstone was wise when he wrote, "Attachment to a Church building is by no means to be dismissed as sentimentality: it may well contain a profound, though possibly inarticulate, understanding of what that building is."[4]

After his death, Francis was paradoxically responsible for the construction of some very large cathedrals. Francis had to be buried somewhere grand, so the pope ordered the construction of the impressive Gothic cathedral San Francesco; today this basilica dominates the skyline of Assisi. Would Francis have grimaced to see such a cathedral devoted to his memory? In heaven, he no doubt smiles more broadly over San Damiano, the modest church he rebuilt with his own hands.

Finishing there, he moved to another, Rivo Torto, then to another, Santa Maria degli Angeli. Down a steep slope, about three miles from San Damiano, there is a sanctuary at Rivo Torto. Inside you find two huts, where Francis slept, ate, taught, and served with the friars in the early years of their ministry. I persuaded our group of teenagers to walk all the way to Rivo Torto, and along the way we were treated to a couple of roosters crowing, sunshine and wind, and the lovely sense of community you get from the rigors of physically walking together. We sat inside and talked about lepers in Francis's day—and the untouchables in our own day.

From there, we walked the road into town, where you can't miss a rather ugly baroque structure near the train station; Cunningham called it "a monument to staggeringly bad taste."[5] You walk inside the bulky building and giggle: right in the middle, on the floor, is the tiny rock chapel that Francis rebuilt, and in which he prayed and around which he served lepers. Simone Weil called it "an incomparable marvel of purity."[6] So sacred is this humble sanctuary that it has not one but two names: Santa

Maria degli Angeli (Saint Mary of the Angels), and then Portiuncula—a nickname Francis devised that stuck, meaning "the little portion."

Perhaps this "little portion," dwarfed by a gaudy structure of a church hiding but then revealing it, is a helpful way to imagine every church. Some exterior is visible to the naked eye. But somewhere at the heart of the church, deep inside, is a small chapel, nothing more than a hut or shack where a few people gathered to pray and hope, a person or two long since dead—and it is their memory, and the intimacy of what is small, that is the reality of every church housed in something more magnificent.

At the epicenter of every church is the living Lord, on a small plate next to a cup, on a table, people gathered around, words overheard, songs sung, the walls finally arching up and over, some kitschy art here and there, an aging organ, a man in a robe, a woman speaking, a choir singing, bulletins, budgets, small rooms with children playing, teenagers slumped through a discussion hour, parking spaces, a sign by the road.

But then Francis would even have loved the hideous baroque church, and instead of criticizing its kitschy tackiness, he would have swept a little and picked up a plastic cup dropped by a tourist, wouldn't he? Ugly churches are beautiful. We need structures of all kinds, and God blessed this institution to bear witness to God, despite its foibles, precisely because of its rickety ramshackleness. "God can carve the rotten wood, and ride the lame horse" (Martin Luther). At the heart of the ugliness of the Church is Beauty, and life pulsates outward, beautifying all of life.

HOW SHOULD THE CHURCH ORGANIZE ITSELF?

Francis heard his call in the Church, from the Scriptures he heard in the Church, before the crucifix that artisans had produced for the glory of the Church. With the direct authority of Jesus himself, you would think Francis would simply launch out and do what Jesus told him to do. But he remained submissive to the Church. He insisted that his friends and followers remain submissive to the Church: "Let all the brothers be, live and speak as Catholics."[7] He journeyed to Rome to meet with the pope, not to tell the pope what was wrong with the Church, but to ask permission to live out what Jesus had envisioned for him, through him.

One of the most memorable frescoes lining the wall of the San Francesco sanctuary portrays a dream that Pope Innocent III had when Francis first visited Rome. Written accounts vary, but in one popular version, Francis knocked on the door of the papal palace at San Giovanni in Laterano. Dressed in the friars' habit, but looking like an impoverished peasant, he was summarily turned away.[8]

But that night, the pope had a dream. The Church—the grand Lateran Church, the pinnacle of the institutional Church, symbolizing all of Christendom—was tipping over, about to fall to the ground. Hoisting it up on his shoulder, preventing its collapse, was a young man, wearing the tunic of a poor laborer. The pope realized it was the disheveled young man who had been turned away the day before. So emissaries were sent to find him and to escort him to the palace. Francis came, met the pope, and told the story of what he was about, asking permission to continue, to formalize this new order of the faithful serving Christ in the Church and world.

How do we conceive the authority of the Church? At times we mistakenly think of the Church as the Phantom of the Opera, teaching Christine to sing, not so she can take wings and fly and thrill audiences, but so she might make music as one imprisoned, only for the benefit of the traditional vested powers. But Francis, who probably struck Church authorities as a bit strange, was not shuttled aside as a threat or sent to the dungeon. His quest was embraced and appreciated by the Church—and might it be precisely because Francis was not a renegade, zealous to bash the Church, but an insider who loved the Church?

Francis's proposal for a new order staggers the imagination. Today, church adjudicatories deal with formal proposals, framed in legal language, adhering to Robert's Rules of Order. We have

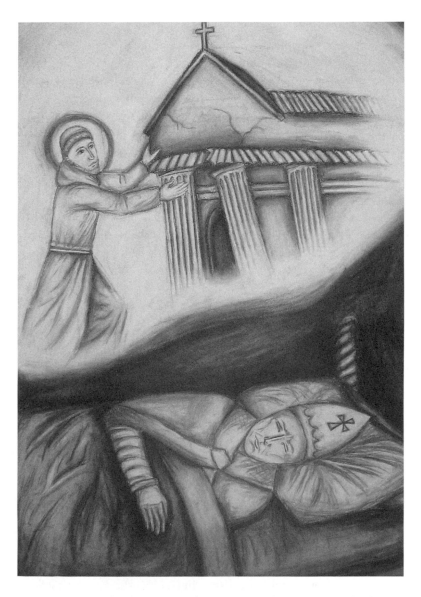

committees, subcommittees, appropriate language, task forces, motions, amendments, voting, recording, and the results read like those books of torts that line the shelves of law offices or else like entrepreneurial strategy pieces.

Happy to follow whatever procedure that would be required, Francis brought a different sort of proposal to the pope. Obviously Francis had no corporate sensibility, no thought-out plan of implementation. All he had scribbled down was a pasting together of various Bible verses about how to live, things Jesus had said to his disciples, instructions straight from the Gospels. The first chapter of his first Rule mandates that the friars are to follow the teaching and footprints of our Lord Jesus Christ, who said,

> If you wish to be perfect, go, sell everything you have and give it to the poor, and you will have treasure in heaven; and come, follow me. And: If anyone wishes to come after me, let him deny himself and take up his cross and follow me. Again: If anyone wishes to come to me and does not hate father and mother and wife and children and brothers and sisters, and even his own life, he cannot be my disciple.[9]

Handing this gathering of Bible passages to the pope, Francis basically said, "Here, we want to go do this."

What's wrong with the Church? Nothing, and the rebuilding of the Church might just hinge on our willingness to be attentive to the Church's true treasure, the things Jesus said and did. Imagine a man offering a proposal to his church council, a woman seeking ordination, a committee bringing forward a new idea, a presbytery or diocese marshaling a ten-year plan—and they pretty much just open their Bibles, read some verses, and say, "Here, we want to go do this."

In Franciscan lore, the most pivotal institutional conference ever held was the so-called Chapter of the Mats in 1221—and if we compare the "mats" event to our denominational meetings, we might gasp over how simple things could be. From astounding distances, men who believed in what Francis was trying to do came home from far-flung mission fields. Priests, laity, stragglers, and even a crowd of lepers filled the valley around the Portiuncula, where they slept on mats on the ground at night, while daytime was given to prayer, worship, and planning. Power plays were frowned upon. Francis himself, obviously the leader, well positioned to run for some hifalutin office, subordinated himself and insisted others take the lead.

Those entrusted with the job of standing up front read from a few pages Francis had written. Notice the simplicity of Francis's words: "The Rule of these brothers is this: to live in obedience, in chastity, and without anything of their own and to follow the teachings and the footprints of Our Lord Jesus Christ." [10] *Footprints* is just about right. The word implies movement, going out, being on a path. For Francis and his friars, Christianity wasn't a still life, but something in motion, with a pace, going someplace. You perspire, and your feet get dirty.

Footprints is also a humble way to speak of imitating Jesus. You are not Jesus; you are not even his feet. From a ways back, you simply follow. You put your foot where it appears his foot was, and then you do it again with your other foot. You need not be perfect, and if you stray off for a bit, you can nose out the tracks once more. The Church does not need to be perfect either.

CAN I BE A CHRISTIAN WITHOUT THE CHURCH?

What would Francis say to us today about the Church? Increasingly people feel they can be closer to God, and serve God more faithfully, apart from the Church, liberated from the dead weight of the Church. Books touting a purer, fresher Christianity outside the Church sell well. Jonathan Campbell, with his wife, Jennifer Campbell, wrote *The Way of Jesus: A Journey of Freedom for Pilgrims and Wanderers*, the story of why they exited organized religion: "Not because we have lost our faith, but to save it. . . . The Church gets in the way of me experiencing Jesus."[11] They want Jesus straight up, not on the rocks.

But don't we get Jesus across a two-thousand-year divide? Weren't the Gospels written within the institution of the Church, and for the Church? Campbell was reared in a devout, Bible-reading home. You have to wonder how people who weren't would ever join a movement to stick to the Jesus who had been housed for so long in the Church now being fled.

People have decent reasons to feel disenfranchised from the Church. We certainly need reform. But hasn't the Church in every epoch acknowledged its own foolishness? The Church's foibles aren't newfangled inventions: we've had centuries of practice! Francis encountered the Church's lostness eight centuries ago. Certainly, the Church is lost; we are unrighteous, as good as dead, as crumbled as San Damiano.

But what if it were otherwise? What would God do with a Church that never lost its way, was fully righteous, was vibrantly "alive" (as so many congregations now boast), totally holy? We will never know. But we do know that God is glorified (although the world may not notice, and many spiritual people may not either) in a Church that is an embarrassment to itself and to God.

Perhaps this is the Church's power. The Church still has power, after all these years. On entering the Portiuncula, Simone Weil felt compelled "by something stronger than I was" to kneel and pray for first time in her life.[12] The Church still bears its treasures—and don't we need them to keep us grounded and accountable? Maybe the power of the Church is in the kneelers, perhaps an embroidered cushion, those pull-down wooden contraptions, or an altar rail. The people at prayer, pleading for forgiveness, seeking God's will despite their awareness they'll never get it done: that is the Church's power.

We kneel and pray in a Church we know needs to be rebuilt. We blush when we notice the embarrassing disconnect between the Church's activities and the words read aloud in the Church. Consider a passage such as Matthew 10, which Francis took literally: sending out his disciples, Jesus said, "Take nothing for your journey . . . no gold, no silver." Isn't Ulrich Luz right?

> Almost never in its history has the church resembled what is here described. . . . The church has not consisted of itinerant radicals; quite the contrary, the radicals, whenever they existed, were considered suspect. . . . The idea of itinerant radicalism disappeared almost entirely. The churches were extremely successful in ignoring it. No wonder: a church that

constructs cathedrals and that offers not only food but both houses and cars to its workers cannot appreciate this kind of tradition. [13]

We may explain away Jesus' words: they applied only way back then; they are impractical; how could we help the poor if we became poor? In a way, this is the same as asking, What would happen if we took the Bible seriously instead of explaining it away? We might press Francis a bit further on how he read the Bible, and how he might help us read the difficult passages and, probably more important, the easy passages.

CHAPTER 5

READING THE BIBLE LITERALLY

One of the most compelling relics that tourists in Assisi can view is the small bound volume of the Gospels Francis carried and read. Looking at it, I cannot fully fathom how much that small book was loved by one man, and I am staggered by its power to fashion a life such as Francis's. If the Church's greatest treasure is its Book, if the Scriptures really are (as Luther conceived it) "the swaddling clothes in which Christ is laid," and if the rebuilding of the Church and our lives is somehow tethered to our reading the Bible and being more alert and responsive to it, we need to ask Francis a few questions about how to read the thing, how to approach Scripture. In the presence of someone like Francis, we simply must ask:

SHOULD I TAKE THE BIBLE LITERALLY?

Francis might blush at your having asked, but then his pristine, clear answer would be, "Of course."

But let us venture back in time to the Middle Ages, when no one took the Bible literally. For medieval readers, the Bible was a mystical warren of symbols and codes. Allegory was the artistic game of biblical interpretation. Babylon wasn't really Babylon;

it signified the Roman Empire. The city of Jerusalem wasn't a place on the map in ancient Palestine but a code for the Catholic Church. The Song of Solomon seemed to speak poetically of the intimacy shared between young lovers, but really it speaks theologically about the love between Christ and his bride, the Church. Theologians expended immense energy, and flashed fantastic imagination, as they plumbed the depths of Scripture, which nowhere meant what it seemed. Hadn't Paul said, "The letter kills, but the Spirit gives life" (2 Corinthians 3:6 NRSV)?

Francis befuddled such clever, theologically shrewd readers by taking the "letter" quite seriously and intuiting that the "Spirit" wasn't some mysterious, clandestine truth hidden underneath the words on the page. For Francis, the "Spirit" was the power of God's presence to enable him and everyone to be not just "hearers" but also "doers" of the Word (James 1:22 RSV).

As we have seen, the gospel story of Christ was not merely something in which Francis believed. The gospel functioned as the script for his life, and he read that script with a startling naïveté. Henri d'Avranches, writing just six years after Francis's death, captured his approach to Scripture in verse:

> Nor will he gloss over anything,
>   but follow the text and faithfully cling
> To every word. Allegory may in much prevail; but the literal
>   sense
> Surpasses it, when no metaphor cloaks the author's mind
> And his words mean what they say.
> Having listened therefore to everything demanded of him,
> As his own interpreter he knows better than to be of the word
> A hearer only and not a doer. He says: "What Christ commands
> I must now do. This is my wish, my vow, what my whole soul
>   desires."[1]

Francis took the Bible literally. He did not decipher it as a code of mysterious intent. He thought that it meant simply what it said—and that he was supposed to do it!

Not long after his primal decision to follow Christ with abandon, Francis went to worship at the tiny chapel of Santa Maria
degli Angeli. In the service he heard Matthew 10:9-10, where
Jesus told his disciples that they should have neither gold nor
coats, neither shoes nor staves for their journey. Glossing over
nothing in this text, Francis became a doer, forsaking fashion and
finery, donning a rough garment girded with a rope instead of a
belt (now fashionable among the clergy as alb and cincture), and
going barefoot (or, as we now say, discalced).

Bernard of Quintavalle, intrigued, invited Francis to his home.
After the evening meal, they retired. Francis pretended to sleep;
Bernard also pretended to sleep, even feigning a snore. Francis
rose and then knelt, praying over and over again, all night long,
"My God, my all." Bernard was touched; he asked Francis the
next morning how to become a servant of God.

The two of them went to a church called San Nicolo, where
Francis asked that the Bible be opened three times at random.
The resulting trio of verses are utterly familiar, yet most of us
never take them seriously: "Sell what you possess and give to
the poor" (Matthew 19:21 RSV); "Take nothing for your journey" (Luke 9:3 RSV); and "If any man would come after me,
let him deny himself" (Matthew 16:24 RSV). Bernard did as
the rich young ruler had not done: he sold everything and
gave it to the poor, as did other young men (Giles, Masseo,
Leo) and even women (especially Clare). Imitating Christ, the
friars became itinerants with no place to lay their heads
(Matthew 8:20).

A couple of years later, Francis trekked to Rome and got an
audience with the pope, Innocent III. As we saw in chapter 4, he
pleaded for the approval of a Rule, a Church-authorized way of
life for him and his fledgling band of brothers. Not only did
Francis fail to produce the kind of denominational handbooks
we're accustomed to (that read like legal briefs); he merely par-
roted the Bible verses that meant so much to him and his friends,
and urged the pope to endorse the clear claims of Scripture, to
take them quite literally, and to join the friars in doing what the
Bible plainly indicated.

MODERN MISREADINGS OF THE BIBLE

How many light-years distant from this is the modern approach to a "literal" reading of the Bible? Christians go to court to demand the teaching of Genesis as science in public schools. Some people lift a verse from Leviticus and rage angrily against gays. "The Bible is clear!" they trumpet, but their manner of life is abjectly unaffected by what the Bible says quite clearly. What might we be doing with our time in imitation of Jesus? How we are to love and not let our souls be poisoned by rancor? Is the Bible a weapon I use to bludgeon somebody else? Or a script I follow for my life?

Then there are those who might benefit from a simple, "literal" reading of the Bible. A brazenly successful attorney visited me in my office and complained that he frankly doesn't read the Bible "because I just can't understand it." I howled out loud: "You are an attorney. You guys specialize in complex language, subtle nuances of words; you write contracts that no nonlawyer could ever decipher, which is precisely why we need lawyers. And you can't understand the Bible?" I started reading a few passages to him. The shrug of "I can't understand the Bible" is a smokescreen, a clever device of avoidance, isn't it? Even Mark Twain mused that the parts of the Bible he couldn't understand didn't trouble him so much as the parts he did understand.

We might ask, "What is God's will for me?"—and while figuring out what God wants me to do may seem mystifying, I have to recognize that you and I could spend our entire lifetimes keeping ourselves busy with the parts of the Bible that are utterly clear and entirely doable: "Do not get drunk" (Ephesians 5:18 RSV); "Judge not" (Luke 6:37 RSV); "Visit orphans and widows . . . keep oneself unstained from the world" (James 1:27 RSV); "The fruit of the Spirit is love, joy, peace, patience, kindness, generosity, faithfulness, gentleness, and self-control" (Galatians 5:22-23 NRSV). It is God's will that we be holy, lift up the poor, reconcile with enemies, avoid gossip, attend worship, clothe the naked, and express gratitude. If you struggle to figure out what God wants, just read the Bible literally. The unmistakable clarity of the vast majority of the Scripture demystifies God's will for me and frankly makes it feel more comprehensive—and daunting!—than merely waiting until a crisis and thinking, *Now I need to know God's will.*

To read the Bible, we need to evaluate *where* we read it and *with whom.* We might read in the den or in bed before falling asleep. We might read in a Sunday school room, chairs circling a table in familiar surroundings. We might read alone, or perhaps my spouse is nearby, or I am in a study group with people I enjoy, people like me. But what if we read—as Francis learned to do!—with strangers, with the poor? And what if we read outside the church building or the comforts of home, at the homeless shelter or under a bridge?

Several years ago we had a Bible study group that spent a session on Jesus' counsel to the rich young ruler: "Sell what you possess and give to the poor" (Matthew 19:21 RSV). After a few guilt-riddled comments, the group eased into some saccharine thoughts: "Jesus is really asking that we be *willing* to give what we have," or "Jesus is suggesting a spiritual disposition in us, giving of my volunteer hours," or "Jesus wouldn't want me to give everything away; I have a family to provide for," or "The poor would probably waste it anyhow," and so forth. They left fairly happy, perhaps sedated a little, but satisfied.

But they had signed up through our church to feed and spend the night with the homeless the following week. One pastor had suggested that our groups read the Bible with our homeless guests. As luck would have it, the group that had dealt so craftily with the rich young ruler found the text for their week with the homeless was none other than "sell what you possess and give to the poor." So confident one week earlier, the group could not bring themselves to say, "Jesus didn't really mean for us to do this," or "I have to provide for my family," or "The poor would probably waste it anyhow."

PERFORMING THE SCORE

Remember the way Francis exemplified Nicholas Lash's thoughts about "performing the Scriptures"—back in chapter 1?[2]

The Bible is a script to be performed; or to expand the image a bit, Bible reading may be compared to what we do with a musical score. We could take the sheet music for a Mozart symphony and sit around a table and point out the F-sharps and shifts in key signature. But the music was written not to be discussed in a room but performed. The players need to pick up their instruments and make music together.

God's Word, the score, exists so we will pick up our instruments, maybe just our hands but probably also our hammers, our cars, our funds, our possessions, and play the thing, act it out, embody the text—and do so together, with other players, not solo. And we play the music as it was written, not inventing our own random symphony as we play along.

Francis had a vivid imagination, as did the early artists who painted his life in those frescoes in sanctuaries all over Italy. Performing the Word, taking the Bible literally in the sense of doing it, begins when we visualize the reality of the text. In the south transept of the basilica of St. Francis we see a painting (by Cimabue) of the crucifixion. At the foot of the cross we see the women, Jesus' mother, Mary Magdalene—and right next to them is Francis. But he didn't live back then . . . or did he?

So common in medieval painting, this vision of me finding myself painted into the biblical story is the starting point of how to read the Bible. It is not that we have a story, virtually a fable or legend from long, long, long ago, and we try by stretching our brains to drag that story across the centuries and "make it relevant" for today. It only seems irrelevant because we cannot yet see. For Francis, what is irrelevant is me and my life today apart from that ancient story. Relevance is there, not here. I do not make the Bible relevant to me; instead, I figure out how to make my life relevant there. How do I find myself in the story?

We do not know precisely or with unfailing accuracy. But we try, we risk a little, we boldly go where at least I have never gone before. Lawrence Cunningham wrote of Francis's whole life as "an ongoing experiment in scriptural exegesis, not at a scholar's bench, but in his gestures, activities, reflections, prayers, acts of charity and preaching. . . . He was a hearer of the Word . . . but most of all, he was a 'Doer' or 'Performer' of the Word."[3] Or as Francis's first biographer put it, "He was no deaf hearer of the gospel; rather he committed everything he heard to his excellent memory and was careful to carry it out to the letter."[4]

With readers like St. Francis, the Word is no longer mere ink on a page, or a word voiced out loud into a room, but becomes life leaping from the page and out of the building. My life can become an open book, my movements the rustling of its pages, and onlookers might see me as a pretty decent interpretation of the Bible, and a tender plea, a fair advertisement to nonreaders to become readers, and then performers themselves.

WHAT IS CHRISTIAN EDUCATION ABOUT?

Educators are figuring out that learning happens not only (and not best!) in a classroom, which can feel unreal and even disembodied, no matter how slick the new technology may be, and maybe even because the technology is so slick. Chemistry happens in the lab, biology out in the field, oceanography under water, medicine in the operating room. Where do we learn theology? What is Christian education all about? And how is our lifelong learning as Christians accomplished? Isn't theological education instilled in practice, in serving, in holiness, in the real world, the one where Jesus walked and Francis labored?

Francis had just a smattering of education. He called himself unlettered (the Latin word he used was, humorously to us, *idiota*!); he knew French, a bit of Latin. Unlike the vast majority of Italians in his era, he knew how to write, and we have relics of his handwriting preserved and on display.

Francis fretted over the danger of books and learning, that friars would get puffed up with intellectual bombast and lose the humility of the servant; books and all that attaches to the academic enterprise would become the new possessions that possess (and just because books and universities might be about the topic of religion does not make them any less risky as possessions!). Paul Sabatier wrote that Francis believed "there will always be enough students for the universities, and that if scientific effort is a homage to God, there is no risk of a lack of this sort of worshiper. But Francis looked in vain about him for those who would fulfill the mission of love and humility."[5]

So how jarring is the undeniable fact that, in the history of scholarship and universities, Franciscans have been among the most brilliant, their pedigree unmatched? Over the centuries, followers of Francis included St. Bonaventure, St. Anthony of Padua, St. Albert the Great, Duns Scotus, William of Ockham, a veritable hall of fame of medieval thought. "That they became chairs at prestigious centers like Paris was exactly what Francis did not have in mind for his companions,"[6] Cunningham wryly suggests.

Bodily discipline was paramount for Francis and his friends. But later generations either couldn't or didn't want to subject their bodies to radical discipleship, so they found a convenient, easier, and more insidious substitute: discipline of the mind.[7] St. Bonaventure, himself a brilliant scholar, wrote the official version of St. Francis's life, purposely omitting what earlier biographers had remembered about Francis's distrust of books, study, and knowledge—and not surprisingly he also cheated a bit and understated Francis's radical views on poverty and money.[8]

Francis invites us to rid ourselves of worldly possessions. Could this conceivably include books? Or even the Bible? There is the old story of the desert monk who had given away all his possessions, save his copy of the Gospels. In order to feed the poor, he sold the book, explaining, "I have sold even the word that commands me to sell all and give to the poor."[9] Francis and his friends were notorious for giving away those beautifully crafted Bibles that adorned churches of their day.

Interestingly enough, when Church history is taught, Francis is rarely mentioned, although he is the towering giant of the Middle Ages. We focus (and perhaps we should) on grand ideas and titanic thinkers, like St. Thomas Aquinas or St. Anselm. But perhaps students should be pressed to pay attention to St. Francis, whose genius wasn't mental analysis or soaring rhetoric. He went down into the valley, got his hands dirty, exhibited a more brilliant grasp of the Scripture and theology than all the thinkers put together—and gave the Bible away.

ST. ANTHONY'S BREAD

During Francis's lifetime, one friar appeared who somehow managed to think as shrewdly as any scholar of his day and yet live as humbly as Francis himself. Anthony of Padua lived in a hermitage under spartan conditions. Once the friars had gathered for a service, and the minister asked if one of them would preach. One by one they declined, feeling unprepared. The minister did not think to ask Anthony because he was considered a simpleton. But finally Anthony stepped forward, and his homily astonished those who heard it: eloquent, undergirded by stellar logic, pulsating with humility and faith.

People began to request him as speaker, writer, scholar. Francis wrote him a letter, reluctantly granting Anthony's wish to write and teach, but only "on the condition that you do not extinguish the spirit of prayer and devotion." [10] To this day, Catholics sponsor collections of food for the poor, called St. Anthony's Bread. How lovely: the most brilliant scholar of his day, one of the official "doctors of the Church," remembered not for his theological acumen so much as for being one who fed the poor.

We read the Bible, and we turn to books—like the one you are reading just now—but we recall Francis's admonition: books are acceptable "on the condition that you do not extinguish the spirit of prayer and devotion." Sometimes we read when we should pray. We talk *about* God instead of talking to God, conversing with God, or listening to God. It is intriguing that Francis, who was uncomfortable with books, wanted to publish his writings—but only his prayers! If he wanted to teach anything that could be written, it would be words to God, praise of God.

Sometimes we read a book about the poor or engage in a mission study, which is a far cry from actually connecting with someone who is poor or going out in mission. Learning is good. Jesus said, "You will know the truth, and the truth will set you free"

(John 8:32 NIV). But "of making many books there is no end, and much study is a weariness of the flesh" (Ecclesiastes 12:12 NRSV). Books of scholarship, commentaries on the Bible, and devotional classics might fail us if we let them become a kind of protective film between the Bible's claim and the student. Those who write about the Bible or about God can usher us toward God and our own encounter with the Scriptures and thus into action, but they also can block our view of the Scriptures or God, and occupation with reading can be an evasion of action. In my life of writing, I hope and pray I am one, and not the other.

How do we read the Bible? We read, slowly, letting its words do their work. We even use our memory to recall the words. But we do not linger long before we spring up and act on the words, finding ourselves in the story, envisioning ourselves, and the next hour and day, in the painting. Francis would insist that our education happens out there, with the poor, in the muddy pigsty. For we are in pursuit of conformity to Jesus, and the goal is not the accumulation of information, but the transformation of the heart and the beauty of handing a hungry person a piece of bread.

CHAPTER 6
THE IMITATION OF CHRIST

Many admirers of St. Francis recognize that he had a bit of a dramatist inside. For all his humility, he lived as if he were on stage, aware people were watching, determined to pull off his experiment in living out the Bible in ways that were not merely faithful but also compelling, interesting, alluring. His was a "virtuoso performance."[1]

So, to this natural born actor, to this incredibly naïve reader and performer of Scripture, I find myself wanting to pose a question we've heard so many times as to make it monotonous—and I have a hunch what his answer might be. The question?

WHAT WOULD JESUS DO?

Francis's answer? I at least hope he would say,
"Watch me."
"Come with me."
Maybe he would be more deferential and humble and would point away from himself. But I wonder. He believed he could exhibit what Jesus was about, and he didn't seem to mind people watching. If we want to know what Jesus would do, if we want to get involved in doing what Jesus would do, perhaps we can learn

a lot by simply watching Francis and trying, however feebly, to do the kinds of things he tried.

The Little Flowers begins by framing its charming tales this way: "We must consider how the glorious Sir Saint Francis was conformed to the blessed Christ in all the acts of his life."[2] To read *The Little Flowers* is to see another Jesus walking the hills of Umbria. Since Francis was "like another Christ given to the world for the people's salvation . . . God the Father willed to make him in many of his actions conformed and similar to His Son, Jesus Christ."[3]

Over time, this tendency to see Francis as Jesus was carried to absurd lengths. Bartholomew of Pisa, in the late fourteenth century, wrote *On the Conformity of the Life of the Blessed Francis to the Life of our Lord Jesus*, a lengthy tome that strains credulity. We read that Francis, like Christ, chose twelve companions, one of whom, Giovanni della Cappella, betrayed and hanged himself. Francis turned water into wine. He healed the blind, the demon-possessed, the lame. So noteworthy were his miracles that throngs pressed toward him, grasping for the hem of his garment. When he entered a city, crowds clapped and rejoiced, tearing branches from trees to wave. He was born not in the five-room house where his wealthy parents surely lived, but in a stable.

Francis's followers clearly got carried away, so determined were they to trace Francis in the shape of Jesus. But think about it: what is the likelihood that, after you die, people who talk about you will remember so many little details in your life that were Christlike that they get a little carried away comparing you to Jesus?

A few years ago, WWJD ("What would Jesus do?") was the jewelry and bumper sticker craze. But have those who sport WWJD bothered to figure out what Jesus really would do? And what then might I do? Am I interested in conformity to Christ or, to phrase it better, in being "transformed" (Romans 12:2 NRSV) by the power of God into somebody who resembles Jesus? Can my mind be reshaped over time so that I might someday be surprised to notice inside my head not my own mind but the mind of Christ (Philippians 2:5)?

How did this mimicking of Christ happen for Francis? He made himself utterly familiar with the stories of Jesus. Francis read the Gospels constantly, listened to them continually, reflected on them all day long. When he heard anything in the story of Jesus, he was incapable of erecting any barriers between Jesus' day and his own, between Jesus' life and his own. As far as Francis was concerned, Jesus did not live twelve centuries earlier. Those fanciful medieval painters were in sync with Francis when they painted thirteenth-century people into scenes from the Bible as if they were there.

For Francis, there was an urgent immediacy to the Bible's accounts, and he accepted the Bible text as his to-do list for the day. Jesus had no place to lay his head and slept out of doors? Francis did the same. Jesus touched lepers? Although it made him shudder at first, Francis found a leper and touched him, and eventually touched many lepers and built a hospital for them with his own hands.

Thomas of Celano summed up everything Francis was about from the time he got up in the morning until he went to sleep at night:

> He was always with Jesus:
> Jesus in his heart,
> Jesus in his mouth,
> Jesus in his ears,
> Jesus in his hands;
> He bore Jesus always in his whole body.[4]

Years ago, I printed those words and stuck them on my refrigerator, next to my phone, and in my top desk drawer. Francis can help us during the day by such a powerful image: Right now, am I with Jesus? Is Jesus in my heart? I am about to say something: Is Jesus in my mouth? I am listening to someone: Is Jesus in my ears? I am picking up something, holding something, reaching out my hand, working with my hands: Is Jesus in my hands? I notice my body, where it is, what it's doing, what I'm putting in it, where it's going: Am I bearing Jesus in my whole body?

If Francis were at dinner and simply heard the name "Jesus," he forgot to eat, or if he were on the road and started singing a song about "Jesus," he would lose his way or forget his destination. Am I ever distracted by Jesus? Am I ever "lost in wonder, love and praise"?[5]

MY LIFE IS MY ARGUMENT

We have a couple of problems, though, don't we? Although I know the English language, and the Bible has been well translated into English so it's as plain as the nose on my face, I still manage to misread Jesus. My vision is selective: I see what I want to see, and ignore what gets under my skin. I reinvent Jesus into somebody more palatable to me. Albert Schweitzer delivered his famous lectures at the University of Strasbourg, helping his students understand how we misread Jesus and transmute him into whomever we want him to be: "Each successive epoch of theology found its own thoughts in Jesus. . . . Each individual created Him in accordance with his own character. There is no historical task which reveals a person's true self as the writing of a Life of Jesus."[6]

But think about Schweitzer! A world-class organist and authority on Bach, philosopher and theologian, perhaps the greatest Bible scholar of his generation, yet also a brilliant physician: Schweitzer took his reading of the Bible seriously and encountered Jesus quite personally. He had written,

> As one unknown and nameless he comes to us, just as on the shore of the lake he approached those men who knew not who he was. His words are the same: "Follow thou me!" and he puts us to tasks which he has to carry out in our age. He commands. And to those who obey, be they wise or simple, he will reveal himself through all that they are privileged to experience in his fellowship of peace and activity of struggle and suffering, till they come to know, as an inexpressible secret, who he is.[7]

So did Schweitzer continue talking about Jesus in the lecture halls of Europe, taking breaks to wow people with his keyboard wizardry? No. He put on a pith helmet and moved into the jungle of Africa to practice medicine among the world's most disadvantaged people. Why? He wrote, "I decided . . . I would make my life my argument. I would advocate the things I believed in terms of the life I lived and what I did."[8] Shallow Christian friends thought he had lost his mind. But he still stands as one of the most exemplary heroes of an entire century, a virtual St. Francis of his day.

But when I think about Schweitzer, I feel the way I do when I think about Francis: in a way, I feel larger; I sense the possibilities. But then I weigh my life, and I just feel so small. And I wonder what causes me to live in such a puny way. I want to imitate Jesus, but my effort feels so toddling, so amateurish. No matter how valiantly I try to be like Jesus, I flounder so embarrassingly. I readily admit that even on my holiest, most spiritual days, I cannot say Jesus is entirely in my heart, mouth, ears, hands, and body.

But Francis always exhibited a tender mercy to his friends, to new converts, and even to himself. Jesus is all mercy, and there is a hidden mercy tucked inside even Francis's biographers' attempts to extol his Christlikeness. Thomas of Celano surveyed Francis's life and concluded,

> His highest aim, foremost desire, and greatest intention was to pay heed to the holy gospel in all things and through all things, to follow the teaching of our Lord Jesus Christ and to retrace His footsteps completely. . . . He scarcely wanted to think of anything else.[9]

Footsteps? I walk behind someone who is great. I do not have to be great. I simply walk behind, try to set each foot down on the ground where the feet in front of me have walked. I am in a shadow of sorts. I do not have to be Francis. I do not have to be Jesus. But I see their footsteps. I could traipse off in some other direction, but I step gingerly where they walked. I am not as good as they were when they pioneered the journey. But I don't have to be.

Francis merely retraced Jesus' footsteps. He was humble, knowing fully well he was no second Christ. Once he set out to fast for forty days but ate half a loaf of bread on the thirty-ninth day so as to avoid any hint of vainglory. Francis followed in Jesus' footsteps. What can I do? I merely retrace Francis's footsteps, which seems safer to me than even trying Jesus' footsteps directly! G. K. Chesterton once made the lovely suggestion that Francis was "a splendid and yet a merciful Mirror of Christ." He continued,

> If St. Francis was like Christ, Christ was to that extent like St. Francis. . . . It is really very enlightening to realise that Christ was like St. Francis. . . . St. Francis is the mirror of Christ rather as the moon is the mirror of the sun. The moon is much smaller than the sun, but it is also much nearer to us; and being less vivid it is more visible. Exactly in the same sense St. Francis is nearer to us, and being a mere man like ourselves is in that sense more imaginable. [10]

Francis is imaginable, and so I venture out and retrace his footsteps.

STARTING SMALL

So I will start small, just as Francis was small, just as God became small in Christ, whose best sermon began with "blessed are the poor in spirit" (Matthew 5:3 NRSV). The Beatitudes, which invite us to see the world turned upside-down, declare that the blessed are the poor, those who mourn, the meek, those who hunger and thirst for righteousness, the pure in heart, the merciful, the peacemakers, even those who are persecuted.

When I wrote a book on the Beatitudes, I suggested that Francis's picture could be attached to any one of these in a Bible dictionary. [11] His threadbare robe, on display for tourists in Assisi, is evidence that he became poor. When he saw the plight of any creature who suffered, he mourned; late in life he had lost most of his vision from so much weeping. Who was ever so hungry and thirsty for righteousness? So merciful was he that he would not step on an ant; Francis "seems to have liked everybody, but especially those whom everybody disliked him for liking."[12] His heart was pure, his peacemaking the stuff of legend. And he was persecuted—with the fiercest venom unleashed against him coming from his own father.

The reason Francis was poor, meek, merciful, and pure was Jesus. Do you sense that, when Jesus spoke the Beatitudes, we overhear something of an autobiographical reflection, as if Jesus is saying, "This is who I am, and so this is what friendship with me looks like, for this is what oneness with God looks like"? Jesus was poor and never owned a home: "The Son of man has nowhere to lay his head" (Matthew 8:20 RSV). He hungered for righteousness: "My food is to do the will of him who sent me" (John 4:34 RSV). Jesus' heart was pure; he was merciful to those despised by society. Jesus said, "I am meek and lowly in heart" (Matthew 11:29 KJV); before Pontius Pilate, Jesus was not belligerent but stood "like a lamb that is led to the slaughter" (Isaiah 53:7 RSV) and said nothing. Jesus' entire mission was to make peace, and he was persecuted for it. And how he mourned: he wept over the city (Matthew 23:37) and sobbed with intensity in the garden of Gethsemane.

Maybe this is where I can begin. Let me see if, with Francis, these simple dispositions of Christ might take root in me. I can cover my ears when blasted with society's conventional wisdom (such as "blessed are those who climb the corporate ladder" or "blessed are the good-looking and well-connected"). I can hang out with the poor to discover my own poverty; I can watch the news and let tears flow instead of letting anger rage; I can stop expecting God to be a possession I own today but let God linger as a presence for which I yearn; I can go to the person with whom I am at war and just talk.

I can begin to imitate Christ. I'll try to trust what St. John Chrysostom preached: "Christ gave thee also power to become like Him, so far as thy ability extends. Be not afraid at hearing this. The fear is not to be like Him."[13] Yes, I'll wobble and fall on my face; but that's the beauty of it, isn't it? And perhaps if I imitate Jesus in even halting ways, someone else might find room to join even me. Ubertino da Casale wrote that Francis's goal "was to reproduce in himself *and in others* those footprints of Christ which had been covered over and forgotten."[14] We help each other to remember, and to follow the footprints together, and therefore humbly.

THE DANCING PREACHER

What would Jesus do? Francis could well say, "Watch me," but with no sense of cockiness or spiritual smugness. Sabatier wrote that Francis's humble sense of being only an imitator of Christ, not a perfect copy, "preserved him from all temptation to pride, and enabled him to proclaim his views with incomparable vigor without seeming in the least to be preaching himself."[15] He did not preach himself, but how did Francis preach? And what was going on with his listeners who were literally dumbfounded and catapulted into action by his speech? We should ask Francis: "What makes a good sermon? What should we be listening for?"

Francis could well be ranked as history's most fascinating preacher. Would that some magic could transport us back in time so we could get a video of him practicing his craft! Eyewitnesses said that his buoyant joy in preaching pervaded his body to the point that his feet moved—as if he were dancing. Spectators remarked that he "made a tongue out of his whole body," with gestures that spoke as resoundingly as his words. His goal in preaching was that he might become a "painting" that gave glory to God. He preached in cathedrals, in the city squares, along the roadside, on the seashore. People literally ran to hear him before he'd slip away to the next village.[16]

Francis was not ordained to preach! He was a layperson, a French troubadour who knew the fabric business. He had received absolutely no training in homiletics. Perhaps he had been exposed to the rudimentary arts of rhetoric when he was a student. But he never seemed to use the classic rhetorical modes of speech. Some who heard him summarized Francis's preaching and the response it ignited:

> Not with enticing words of human wisdom, but in the doctrine and virtue of the Holy Spirit he proclaimed the Kingdom of God with great confidence; as a true preacher, confirmed by Apostolic authority, he never used flattering words and he despised all blandishments; what he preached to others in words, he had first experienced by deeds, so that he might speak the truth faithfully. The power and truth of his language, which no man had taught him, made even cultured and learned men marvel, and many hastened to see and hear him, as though he were a man of another century.[17]

He *was* a man of another century: in his heart, and in all that he did, he lived in the Bible's century, and in order to communicate clearly across such a divide of time, he had to use simple, direct, compelling words.

Typical sermons in the Middle Ages treated complex theological issues analytically, as if engaging in scholarly debate. But Francis had never attended one of the great theological universities, so he was not equipped to preach in an academic style. His sermons were all passion, all fervor, a first-person witness by someone whose life had been transformed.

Today, many young Christians sport posters supposing that Francis said, "Preach the gospel; use words if necessary." We have no record that Francis said such a thing, and he used words constantly. But all who were riveted by his preaching claimed that what was most compelling about his talk was that it was matched by his life. There was no dissonance between the things he spoke and the observable habits of his life. Perhaps we might encourage our preachers to be good, to be holy, and for us together to be good and holy so we might hear God's Word. Perhaps instead of letting ourselves be amused by slick talkers, we might look for simpler words coming from the lips of someone who has embodied what the faith is about.

In his intriguing biography of Francis, Michael Robson begins his analysis of the saint's preaching with this sentence: "After his conversion experience . . . Francis began to preach penance to all with great fervour of spirit and joy of mind, edifying his hearers with his simple words and his greatness of heart." [18] The notion of preaching penance "with great fervour" may conjure up images of some hellfire and brimstone hollering. But Francis preached penance "with great fervour of spirit *and joy of mind, edifying* his hearers." We do not associate repentance and joy. Before hearing Francis, no one else had either! Most medieval sermons called for repentance, but the tone was harsh. Sermons felt like a drill sergeant berating a soldier who had marched out of step. Francis knew sin, and grieved his own profusely, weeping visibly over even slight deviations from God's holy will. But there was something playful, hopeful, delightful about his sorrow over his waywardness from God. The joy of repentance is the awareness that God is merciful, that God is love, that power is being unleashed to create newness out of what was stale, ugly, and dying.

Francis exhibited "greatness of heart." Mother Teresa often said that prayer enlarges the heart. Francis's heart was enormous, a vast cavern with room for praise, room for strangers, room for abundant love, room for charity, room for all creation, room for even the infinitely majestic and massive God. Prayer made his heart big. Before preaching, he would spend the entire night in intense prayer. His intimacy with God was not faked or snatched up in the brevity of a quickie prayer. He had spent much time with God in deep conversation.

The subjects treated in his preaching were controversial, even offensive. Times were tense; wars were waged over little tiffs; everybody was armed; knights were heroes. In such a bellicose environment where war was, quite frankly, popular, Francis preached peace. He was too naïve to separate Church and state. To him, God was too large, too pervasive, too involved in the minutiae of the universe to get boxed out of things political. He walked into the teeth of danger and spoke directly to warmongering politicians in Assisi, Perugia, Bologna, and even the Middle East. We will speak with Francis about his legendary peacemaking efforts later. But for the moment, we note that his heroic labors to make peace earned him the right to talk of peace, which he did among people who previously had expended energy only on figuring out how to win wars.

His personal sanctity was not cloaked in his preaching, but was utilized to persuade. Once he rose up from a horrific illness, riddled with fever, and removed his tunic so people could see his sorry appearance, how he had fasted at length as Jesus did, how he had wept over his sins. He took a bowl of ashes, dumped them on his head, and scattered them around the sanctuary. That was the sermon. Those who gathered to "hear" his sermon were moved. His regimen of total devotion to Christ, his implacable commitment to the gospel life, and his evident humility clashed with their flimsy piety, their affluent self-indulgence, their pompous pride. The contrast shamed them, and they were moved to repentance. Joyful repentance, we might imagine.

THE WOUNDS OF JESUS

The heart of Francis's preaching, and of his life, and of the Church and my life and yours, is the cross. Toward the end of his life, Francis had become obsessed with the crucifixion of Jesus, with his suffering for us. Often people would find him standing by the road, weeping. Why? He was simply thinking as he walked along of Jesus' agony on the cross, of Jesus' intense love, of Jesus' physical pain—and he was overcome with grief. "Indeed, so thoroughly did . . . the charity of the Passion occupy his memory that he scarcely wanted to think of anything else." [19] After all, his first conversations with Jesus had taken place as he knelt before a cruxifix. Francis's focus was on the hour when Jesus suffered and yet simultaneously exhibited God's immense grace and glory.

Two years before his death, Francis withdrew from the crowds to rocky Mt. LaVerna. It was September 1224, when the Catholic calendar featured the Feast of the Exaltation of the Cross. He prayed intently, with words of unmatched theological power:

> My Lord Jesus Christ, I pray You to grant me two graces before
> I die: the first is that during my life I may feel in my soul and

in my body, as much as possible, that pain which You, dear
Jesus, sustained in the hour of Your most bitter Passion. The
second is that I may feel in my heart, as much as possible,
that excessive love with which You, O Son of God, were
inflamed in willingly enduring such suffering for us sinners. [20]

What happened next is either sheer miracle or a horribly flawed
fabrication. An angelic seraph, nailed to a cross—or was it Christ
himself?—flew down and pierced the hands, feet, and side of
Francis. For the remaining two years of his life, he was marked by
these wounds, the stigmata. Although he tried to hide them, a
few friends caught a glimpse now and then. The wounds bled
intermittently, but Francis never complained. When his corpse
was prepared for burial, the stigmata were uncovered and certi-
fied as genuine. Since that time, history has known other stig-
matics, holy believers who suffer medically unexplainable
wounds in their hands, feet, and sides that bleed periodically.[21]

What would Jesus do? What did Jesus do? Jesus let himself be
treated brutally. He was mocked, slapped, flogged. He let his holy,
beautiful body endure the most gruesome physical torment of
crucifixion. Large iron nails were driven through his flesh and
bone into a shaft of olive wood. A lance pummeled his abdomen.
Thorns pressed into his forehead. We avoid suffering at all costs,
but what does it cost us? We never know the heart of God, and
the profound love of God, until we enter into his wounds.

During Holy Week, I took a handful of teenagers to visit
LaVerna, a daunting, rocky zone, with precipitous cliffs.
According to legend, Francis was climbing the mountain and col-
lapsed in exhaustion and thirst. Miraculously, water spouted from
the rocks, and a flock of birds gathered to sing. Francis climbed
higher; we climbed too. There are dozens of caves and crevices,
and on this craggy terrain, Francis imaginatively felt he was
entering the wounds of Christ; some call LaVerna "a wounded

mountain."[22] Francis believed that the earthquakes that accompanied the crucifixion of Christ created the rugged landscape.

Stops along the way of our climb included several small chapels. The Chapel of the Relics exhibits a tablecloth, bowl, and cup Francis used when he was there. A small piece of linen is thought to be stained with Francis's own blood; and then there is the very garment Francis wore when he received the stigmata. Francis was wounded from on high, or from within, a searing testimony of the saint's physical intimacy with his Savior.

Paul spoke obliquely about carrying "the marks of Jesus" on his body (Galatians 6:17 NRSV). To be marked with Jesus: it is as if Jesus wrote, "What wondrous love is this?" onto the very body of Francis. Why was Francis chosen for this miracle? Was his devotion to Christ more passionate than mine? Do I want to go so far? Why did God choose Francis? One day, when Francis returned from praying, Brother Masseo asked,

> "Why you? Why you? Why you? The whole world seems to be coming after you, and everyone is seeking to see you, to hear you, and to obey you: you are not a handsome man; you are not a man of great knowledge or wisdom; you are not of noble birth! Why does the whole world come to you?"
> Francis replied that God could not find a greater sinner, or one "more unqualified and more vile. And therefore, to perform this miraculous deed which he intends to perform . . . he chose me." [23]

God's great deeds wrought in Francis's life extended to the natural world, and even throughout the known world of his day. Nothing is as noteworthy as the way Francis dealt with pain, suffering, and evil in this world.

CHAPTER 7
PEACE FOR CREATION AND HUMANITY

We might wish to ask Francis our perennially thorny question about the causes of evil: "Why do bad things happen?" But Francis never went there. A saint who seeks out suffering, who wants to hurt the way Jesus hurt, isn't likely to wonder about why bad things happen—as if pain is some anomaly alien to God.

Nothing startles us so much as the realization of the way Francis responded to everything he had going on during the winter of 1224–25. Physically he was miserable: nearly blind, his lungs riddled with tuberculosis, in constant pain, exhausted from the cumulative effects of fasting and rigorous travel, mice infesting the house, emaciated by sporadic bleeding from gaping wounds in his hands, feet, and side, with the only medical attention available being of the medieval sort that did more harm than good. Professionally he was stricken: the friars were bickering, in constant turmoil, showing every sign of the eventual ruin of his movement. Emotionally he was drained.

And yet, instead of sinking into despondency, instead of pleading with God to alter his fate, to fix all that was broken in and around him, Francis pleaded with the Lord not to cure him but to help him bear his illnesses patiently. God's reply? Francis "was told in spirit" he would receive a "great and precious treasure," and a promise to "be glad and rejoice in your illness and troubles because as of now, you are as secure as if you were already in my kingdom."[1]

That treasure, Francis's gladness, his joyful security, began to take shape in consonants, vowels, syllables, with a musical note, a phrase, a melody. His trembling, aching hands took up a pen and began to write a marvelous poem, a song of immense, personal praise, an invitation to all of us to rejoice in the delights of God's kingdom:

> Be praised, my Lord, for all your creatures.
> . . . for the blessed Brother Sun
> who gives us the day and enlightens us through You. . . .
> Be praised, my Lord, for Sister Moon and the stars
> Formed by You so bright, precious, and beautiful. [2]

And so began history's most soaring paean of praise to God, poetry's proudest moment, Christianity's purest exposition of our devotion to the works of God: Francis's Canticle of the Creatures. Facing the worst, he burst forth with praise, living as the textbook example of a theological truth I overheard a wise friend declare a few years ago: "The antidote to despair is praise."

What kind of faith enables someone to rise up like a phoenix from the ashes of despair and give voice to the wonder of God and the grandeur of God around us, the delicate embroidery of loveliness with which God has graced the universe and our lives? We may recall the apostle Paul and his friend Silas singing hymns in the Philippian jail at midnight (Acts 16), and then Paul's resplendent letter to his friends in Philippi, pulsating with joy—written while shackled to a guard in a Roman prison! Consider his phrases:

> I thank my God upon every remembrance of you. . . .
> What has happened to me has really served to advance the
> gospel. . . .
> Yes, and I shall rejoice. . . .
> Christ will be honored in my body. . . .
> If there is any encouragement in Christ . . . complete my joy. . . .

> Even if I am to be poured as a libation . . . I am glad and rejoice.
> . . .
> For his sake I have suffered the loss of all things. . . .
> Rejoice in the Lord always. . . . Let all men know your
>   forbearance. . . .
> I have learned, in whatever state I am, to be content.[3]

If you want to host a Bible study of Philippians, look to the last year and a half of Francis's life, and you will understand precisely what Paul is talking about.

Holding in our minds Francis's fragile health and endurance of pain, let us step back and consider the way he extolled nature and reflect with him over a few questions.

YOU'RE A LIBERAL ON THE ENVIRONMENT, RIGHT?

We feel like we needn't ask Francis about saving the planet, as we assume he would be very "green," that he would join protest lines against nukes and global warming, that he would be a nemesis to industries that threaten rainforests or wetlands, that he would drive a hybrid (or ride a bike), that he would stand in front of a bulldozer to protect an animal habitat, that he would recycle, that he would hug a few trees before breakfast each day.

Perhaps. But there is a surprising wrinkle in the way Francis loved nature. With his sense of irony he would laugh at our question and reply, "Liberal? Not in the least. I am conservative on the environment. Unlike modern-day conservatives, I want to *conserve* nature—but not for the reasons you think. And there is so much about nature and the world you're missing because you're obsessed with cordoning off a secure place for yourself and your grandchildren."

For Francis, nature isn't about us. The sun isn't something we hope will come out from behind the clouds so we can enjoy the ball game or provide nice lighting for my photography outing. The sun is my brother, a ball of immense energy God tossed into the Milky Way to give light. The moon isn't something to ignore most nights like the rest of God's starry host, lost to the ambient, phony light of our cities. The moon is my sister, precious, fair. Like my children when they were two and three years old, we glance out the window toward the shimmering light, close the book, and say "Goodnight, moon."

We are siblings, the sun, the moon, the light, even the dark. And God is our Father. This personal relationship, this sense of kinship, is what we have lost over many centuries of building, paving over paradise, stringing up things electric. We are dishonored because we have forgotten how to honor everything God has made. In the age of chivalry, Francis employed the graceful, "courtly mode of address" while speaking to creatures; Roger Sorrell called this "Francis's unique way of showing his high regard for creatures by giving them the same type of chivalric honors he also gave to his human 'companions of the Round Table.'"[4]

Of course, Francis did not stumble on this recognition of nature only at the sunset of his life. For years he had not only spoken adoringly *about* flowers. He spoke *to* the flowers, and encouraged them, as though they could understand, to praise the Lord. When walking by a field, he would turn and address stalks of corn, hilly meadows, a running brook, and even the wind rustling through the trees, exhorting them to serve and praise God joyfully. Francis once saw a gardener pressing seed into a newly plowed plot; to this stranger he said, "Do not plant it all with vegetables, but leave a bit of ground free so that there will be wild plants which produce our sisters the wildflowers."[5]

Of course, Francis saw the animal kingdom as an extended family of siblings in God's kingdom: birds, cows, chimpanzees, elephants, all our siblings. Come to think of it, science has been trying to teach this to religious people, who resist the lovely truth of our kinship, our physiological interconnectedness with all God's creatures. The modern discovery that the chimpanzee is my close cousin would have tickled Francis's fancy; if told we had descended from some common primate, Francis would slap his knee and say, "I knew it!"

To this day, stone bird feeders memorialize Francis's care for living creatures, although most gardeners who own such statues never understand the depth of his union with them. Walking along a road just south of Assisi, Francis and his friars noticed a bevy of birds chirping loudly. When the others wanted to wave them away or hush them, Francis spoke to them instead; he actually preached to them, a sermon remembered in one of the most famous frescoes from the Middle Ages:

> My brother birds, you should greatly praise your Creator, and love Him always. He gave you feathers to wear, wings to fly, and whatever you need. God made you noble among His creatures and gave you a home in the purity of the air so that, though you neither sow nor reap, He nevertheless protects and governs you without your least care.[6]

The birds raised their wings and chirped in approval. In later versions, he addressed the birds as his "sisters," and reminded them that God gave them trees for nests, and warned them against the sin of ingratitude.[7]

Other friars followed suit. Francis's companion, St. Anthony, preached to some fish:

> My brother fish, you have a great obligation to give thanks to your Creator, who has given you such a noble element for your home. You have fresh or salt water, as you like. He has given you an element that is clear and transparent, and food to eat by which you can live. When there was the Flood . . . God preserved only you without harm. He has given you fins so you can go anywhere you please. By the command of God you were allowed to preserve Jonah the prophet. You presented the tax-coin to our Lord Jesus Christ. You were the food of the Eternal King Jesus Christ before the Resurrection and after it.[8]

To see every creature and its relationship, not to me and my lifestyle, but to God and the story of Scripture: this is wisdom.

GIVING GLORY TO GOD

But to preach to birds? And fish? Cynics will scoff. Birds cannot understand human speech; fish do not even have ears. But don't you hope that through some miracle of the One who made the birds, the fish, and this crazy preacher, they did hear? And even if they didn't, the friars heard, and we overhear, and somehow Francis's speech to the birds urging them to gratitude, and taking note of God's tender care for them, changes me and how I think, not just about birds, but my own existence under the sky, the water I drink, the clothing I wear.

Thomas Merton wrote,

> A tree gives glory to God by being a tree. . . . It "consents," so to speak, to His creative love. It is expressing an idea which is in God . . . and therefore a tree imitates God by being a tree.
>
> The more a tree is like itself, the more it is like Him. If it tried to be like something else which it was never intended to be, it would be less like God and therefore it would give Him less glory. . . .
>
> For me to be a saint means to be myself. Therefore the problem of sanctity and salvation is in fact the problem of finding out who I am and of discovering my true self.
>
> Trees and animals have no problem. God makes them what they are without consulting them, and they are perfectly satisfied.
>
> With us it is different. God leaves us free to be whatever we like.[9]

If a tree glorifies God nimbly, more effortlessly than I do, then perhaps I might just want to hug that tree, and to keep some developer from chopping it down. If we raze a forest and replace it with a shopping mall, would anyone ever say, "A mall gives glory to God by being a mall"?

Francis would ask us to weep with him when any species is declared extinct, for that is one less voice in the great chorus of praise to God the Creator of every species. To diminish the praise of God is a nefarious business, for how dastardly is it when our world gradually loses its voice of praise? So we protect plants and animals and the good creation in which they live and move and have their being not for our sake, or even for the sake of the world, but for God.

Can we discern connections, as Francis did, between nature and the biblical story, which too often we rend from nature? Francis once thought,

> If I ever speak to the Emperor, I will beg and persuade him, for the love of God and of me, to enact a special law forbidding anyone to catch or kill our sister larks or do them any harm. Likewise, all mayors and lords of castles and villages should be bound to oblige people each year on the day of the Nativity of the Lord to scatter wheat and other grain along the roads . . . so that our sister larks and other birds may have something to eat on such a solemn feast. Also, out of reverence for the Son of God whom the most blessed Virgin Mary on that night laid in a manger between an ox and ass . . . whoever has an ox and an ass be bound on that night to provide them a generous portion of the best fodder. Likewise, on that day, all the poor should be fed good food by the rich.[10]

Francis makes me wonder whether there is some politician to whom I should speak about the birds or at least the poor.

We can see now that Francis's love for nature, his passion for the world and its creatures, has little in common with our political issues. Francis cared deeply for the world and everything in it because he cared for its Creator. Bonaventure wrote of Francis: "Everything incited him to the love of God, he exulted in all the works of the Creator's hands. . . . He admired Supreme Beauty in all beautiful things."[11] He sought to love God in all things, not just in some things, or in obviously religious things, but in everything. The earth, skies, waters, and things that grow are the theater of God's glory. No greater testimony exists to the goodness and greatness of God. I do not know if Francis had ever heard of St. Ephrem, but he would have admired his notion of the "three harps of God": the Old Testament, the New Testament, and nature itself.

BEAUTY TRANSFORMING

Francis may have been wired in such a way that, even before his conversion to an intense relationship with Christ, he admired the wonders of the world. The change he experienced was perhaps this: that his love for the beauty of nature "was transformed into a love of the beauty of God. God was Beauty, and made everything beautiful. Francis began to see beauty even in ugliness."[12] Doesn't the gospel lure us into this same kind of vision, to see beauty in ugliness? God came down in the perfect human form: "Fairest Lord Jesus . . . Beautiful Savior."[13] But they flogged him and pressed thorns into his brow; they nailed him to a wooden cross and pierced his side with a spear.

> He had no form or comeliness that we should look at him,
> and no beauty that we should desire him . . .
> as one from whom men hide their faces he was despised.
> (Isaiah 53:2-3 RSV)

Yet in this ugliness we perceive the stunning beauty of our God.

Francis understood, since his own body was now wretched, and his hands, feet, and side bled spontaneously. His intimacy with the crucified Jesus was precisely what drew him into the deepest conceivable appreciation for nature. Didn't nature itself recoil in horror when Jesus suffered? Francis reflected on all this and believed that when Jesus died, all nature grieved his passing. The cross of Christ became the scaffolding on which Francis hung his adoration of the flowers: he protected the flowers "out of love for Him Who is called The Rose in the plain and the Lily on the mountain slopes"; he spared trees "out of love for Christ, who willed to accomplish our salvation on the wood of the cross."[14]

Could it be that we remain distant from Christ to the degree that we fail to notice and adore the created wonders of nature? And that we never understand the glory of nature until we draw close to the crucified heart of Jesus? In the year 1305, after praying at LaVerna, the very place where Francis received the stigmata, Ubertino da Casale wrote these insightful words about Francis:

> Through looking on things of beauty he would contemplate the Beautiful; in frail creatures he could recognize the infirmities which Jesus in His goodness bore for our salvation. He

made a ladder of every thing, by which he could reach the One
he loved. Altogether special, however, was the love for Christ
crucified which had such a recurrent transforming effect that
he bore, not only in mental attitude but in bodily appearance,
the likeness of the crucified Jesus. [15]

Can everything be a ladder? What about turmoil and strife
among nations? Or in our homes and souls? Since Francis is
known as a peacemaker, we need to ask:

CAN THERE EVER BE PEACE IN THE WORLD?

Since Francis is associated not only with nature, but also with
the whole idea of peace, I have a burning desire to transport him
across the centuries and ask if peace is even possible in our world,
which feels so much more complex and random than his. And if
he should plead for peace, I would most certainly ask him for
some details on how, some strategy, where to begin, and what to
do next. Can there ever be peace in the world?

In the year leading up to his death, Francis had penned the
Canticle of the Creatures, and he and his friends were praying it,
singing it daily, when one day he added a verse, instructing the
friars to sing the newly expanded version in the city square where
the bishop and the mayor would be on a certain day. The two
most powerful men in the city had heard the Canticle many
times, but their ears perked up when they realized a stanza had
been added—quite transparently for their benefit. They had
fallen into belligerence with one another, waging a war of words
that seemed irresolvable. The friars finished their song, and then
these two authorities, to everyone's surprise, met in the middle,
and with "great kindness and love they embraced and kissed each
other."[16]

The added verse? Right after the familiar praise for Brother
Sun, Sister Moon, Brother Wind, Sister Water, Brother Fire, and
Sister Earth, the mayor and bishop heard this:

Be praised, my Lord,
for those who pardon through Your love
and bear witness and trial.
Blessed are those who endure in peace
for they will be crowned by You, Most High.[17]

How do you heal a quarrel between stubborn people? Francis could have accosted them and said, "I think the bishop is right and the mayor is a numbskull," or "Religion and politics don't mix, so just avoid each other," or even "Get along, or God will punish you." Instead, he spoke to neither of them; he spoke to God and offered up a paean of praise that underlined the elusive truth that reconciliation really is the work of God, a gift only the Most High can give. He reiterated a truth we've considered earlier, that the antidote to all kinds of human turmoil is praise: the fix for conflict isn't this or that technique we employ between one another, but turning to God in praise. Then, mysteriously (but then, it's not entirely baffling, is it?), reconciliation dawns.

Can there be peace? We think might makes right, we bet on the guy with the weapons, and we are pretty quick to dismiss those who fancy peace as weak, deluded, unrealistic liberals. But let us remember that Francis was a soldier. He had donned armor and led citizens into battle. He was wounded and today would be awarded a purple heart or two. Francis lived during the Crusades, when the brightest and best young men of Europe "took up the cross": emblazoned on their chests as they ventured out to the battlefield was the sacred symbol of our faith. Francis had worn the military's regalia, but somehow he intuited a revolutionary, creative way to "take up the cross," more akin to the way Jesus took up his cross, and he walked into places of strife—and peace happened.

For Francis, peace wasn't about peace so much as it was about Jesus. To be near Jesus, or like Jesus, you are recruited into the waging of peace. Francis gave away his possessions to be close to Jesus—and isn't there a hint at how to make peace in his divestment? Isn't political strife—and isn't all war at the end of the day—about the protection of or pursuit of some possession, some piece of property, or just plain money itself?

Perhaps you have heard that St. Francis hatched the idea of organizing manger scenes and pageants at Christmas; what is not so obvious is that he was pointing the way to political peace. When Christmas drew near in 1223, he secured the help of a friend in Greccio: animals were herded in, torches were lit, and the people rehearsed the story of Christmas. Thomas of Celano captured the moment in an elegant phrase: "Out of Greccio is made a new Bethlehem." [18] Before we exhale a sentimental sigh, notice the political weight of the manger scene. Crusaders were at that very moment campaigning to crush those who occupied the Holy Land; they wanted to control Bethlehem militarily. But since Bethlehem now can be anywhere, even in Italy, then there is no longer any need to travel to the Holy Land to fight for it. [19]

Our three best stories about Francis involve peacemaking. The first was one my children loved enough that we developed a little puppet show, a reenactment of the day Francis arrived to visit friends in the village of Gubbio. The city gates were bolted shut, the citizens armed with knives and fierce looks. A wolf had been terrorizing the village. He had actually devoured several citizens of Gubbio! When a posse would venture up into the hills, the wolf would hide or manage to eat one of his pursuers. Francis said, "I must pay a visit to my brother the wolf." The citizens offered him weapons, but he climbed the hills unarmed, the citizens atop the city wall witnessing what they were sure would be the end of him.

Sure enough, the wolf appeared, snarling, drooling, baring his fangs. Just as he approached Francis, the saint made the sign of the cross. The wolf sat down. Francis spoke: "Brother Wolf, you do much harm in this area. . . . You are worthy of the gallows as a thief and the worst of murderers. But I, Brother Wolf, want to make peace between you and these people." [20] He urged the wolf to repent, and the wolf bowed his head in sorrow. Francis continued, noticing the barren ground and lack of food on the hillside: "I know very well that you did all this harm because of hunger." The wolf looked up. Francis promised a deal: if the wolf would confess his sin, and promise not to terrorize the people any longer, the people would feed the wolf every day. Francis reached down, and the wolf offered his paw in return.

At first the citizens of Gubbio were suspicious and on their guard. But after some time they began to trust the wolf. Brother wolf came in and out of their homes at his leisure. He was like a pet to them. Even the dogs did not bark at him. Two years later, when he died, the citizens of Gubbio wept. And in 1873, workers repairing a stone flooring uncovered a wolf's skull, elaborately buried beneath a chapel dedicated to St. Francis. Carlo Carretto wisely concluded that the surprise is "not that the wolf grew tame, but that the people of Gubbio grew tame."

The miracle of that morning in Gubbio was not the conversion of the wolf; it was the conversion of the people who lived in Gubbio—who for a fleeting instant believed that a dangerous wolf could be overcome with the gift of food instead of pointed weapons.[21]

BLESSED ARE THE PEACEMAKERS

Seem too fanciful? Prefer a story where Francis talks with people instead of wild carnivores? Once three wicked thieves demanded food at the door of the friars' house in Monte Casale. Cognizant of their shady reputation, the guardian harshly sent them away. Soon Francis arrived and heard of the encounter. "They would be brought back to God more easily by sweetness than by cruel rebukes."[22] He reminded the guardian that Jesus had said, "It is not the healthy who need a doctor, but the sick, and that He did not come to call the just but to call sinners." Francis compelled the guardian to find the robbers and carry several loaves of bread and a jug of wine to them, and to invite them to return as his guests. We are unsure who felt more awkward, the guardian or the thieves. Suspicion yielded to remorse and then reconciliation. Back at Monte Casale they were received with joy and mercy—and after a few weeks all three became friars in Francis's order.

Another story, of compelling pertinence in our world rife with tension between East and West, between the Arab and Western worlds: Francis surprisingly joined a horde of soldiers and knights, led by Leopold of Austria and John of Brienne, in the Fifth Crusade against Islamic Arabs in the Middle East. Arriving at Damietta in Egypt late in the summer of 1219, the crusaders were arrayed in battle-ready formation.

Barefoot, with no shield or sword, Francis walked bravely across no-man's-land toward the Arab army. Drawing their sabers, the Muslims thought to kill him. But he was so pitiful, so defenseless, that they spared him, leading him to the sultan, Malik el-Kamil, who became intrigued with the faith of this unarmed combatant. The sultan reportedly told him, "Brother Francis, I would willingly convert to the faith of Christ, but I am afraid to do it now, because if these people learn of it, they would immediately kill you and me and all your companions." [23] A brief period of peace was won, and the sultan gave Francis a lovely gift: an oliphant, a tusk made into a silver and ivory horn used to call the sultan's army to the hunt or battle. Francis treasured it and used it when he was back home to call the friars together for prayer. Today, visitors to the basilica of Assisi can see it, preserved behind glass. Could it be a sign of the way to peace today?

A few years ago, in response to a sermon on "blessed are the peacemakers," a parishioner e-mailed me, explaining how unrealistic and irresponsible *passivism* is. Now perhaps what I saw on the computer screen was merely a spelling error. But I suspected that this person, who is hardly alone, thought of *pacifism* as *passivism*, that somehow *peace* suggests that we do absolutely nothing, that we be passive in the face of evil. But Jesus didn't say do nothing; he said do something. *Pacifism* means to "make" peace. Jesus said, "Blessed are the doers of peace, the makers of peace." To do peace, to make peace, you have to get busy, you have to act; you have a world of work ahead of you.

Perhaps an extraordinary act is required. Francis walked across no-man's-land; he gave wine and bread to thieves. Remember when King Saul was in murderous pursuit of David? By chance, David happened upon Saul asleep in a cave. Instead of seizing the opportunity to kill him, David engaged in an extraordinary act: he spared Saul even though David was only endangering himself by sparing the king (1 Samuel 24—and again in 1 Samuel 26). The extravagant gesture, the refusal to wield power, the exhibition of startling tenderness: this is the beginning of peace. Dietrich Bonhoeffer said, "There can only be . . . peace when it does not rest on lies and injustice." And then, in the same sermon, he added, "The forgiveness of sins still remains the sole ground of all peace." [24] We tell the truth; we labor for justice; we forgive.

What is forgiveness except the enactment of God's love, and seeing the other person as God sees that person? Francis knew how to love. G. K. Chesterton wrote that Francis seemed "to have liked everybody, but especially those whom everybody disliked him for liking." And again, "Francis had all his life a great liking for people who had been put hopelessly in the wrong." [25] Couldn't peace begin if we could like somebody we're disliked for liking? Or the one hopelessly in the wrong? Do I like anybody others dislike me for liking?

Lepers came to him. No physician would touch them, but Francis treated his "brothers in Christ" with tenderness, treating their wounds, embracing and kissing those who had been ostracized from society, even building a hospital for them. One leper was especially rude and impatient, wearing down the goodwill of even the most loving friars, who were about to throw him out. But Francis intervened and tended to the man himself. He drew a warm bath for him, sprinkled it with special herbs, and prayed intently, taking care of the man for weeks thereafter. A double miracle occurred: the man was healed not only of his leprosy, but also of his nagging.

Francis repeatedly took off his meager garments and gave them to the poor. His love for the poor was tender, generous. "He used to view the largest crowd of people as if it were a single person, and he would preach fervently to a single person as if to a large crowd." [26] If Francis met someone on the road carrying a load, he would insist on bearing it on his own shoulders.

Murray Bodo summarized Francis's formula for peace: "You have to come out from behind your defenses and risk embracing what is seemingly repulsive and dangerous. Only then will there be peace and only love can make it happen." [27] Francis left the security of life behind the walls of Assisi and lived outside, in the open, where safety ranked far lower than finding new friends. Jonathan Sacks, urging us to relish differences among people, asked, "Can we hear the voice of God in a language, a sensibility, a culture not our own? Can we see the presence of God in the face of a stranger?" [28]

And we do not merely cope with the stranger if he or she happens to show up. "Tolerance" isn't a Christian virtue. We seek out the stranger, the leper. We are servants, humble, ready to drop everything to honor somebody else, anybody else who has a need; we don't wait to be asked to help; we seek out opportunities to serve those who haven't thought to ask just yet.

For something "natural" is coming our way, and the question is whether we will be ready to welcome the most unwanted stranger: death itself. Suffering intensely, Francis welcomed what we shrink from, his own death, as have so many martyrs and great saints who knew they were about to be welcomed into God's eternal presence. We marvel at the way Francis died in such unified oneness with nature.

> Be praised, My Lord, for our sister, bodily death
> Whom no one living can escape.
> Woe to those who die in sin!
> Blessed are those who discover thy holy will
> The second death will do them no harm. [29]

CONCLUSION

And now we have come to the end, or at least for now. There is much more to be said, and our relationship with Francis will continue. Part of me drifts into a guilty mood when I think of Francis and his excellence of faith and life. But then I remember that Francis was "relentless with himself," as Leonardo Boff put it, but "not so with his brothers."[1] One friar tried to join Francis in a fast of forty days, but it was so hard. One night he was curled up, crying, trying but unable to sleep. Francis heard him and brought him a loaf of bread, which the two of them shared.

I can never be sure whether to be comforted or challenged by Francis's dying words—and perhaps I should be comforted *and* challenged. Francis did not say, "Do what I did." Instead he said, "I have done what was mine to do; may Christ teach you what you are to do."[2] We follow the One he followed, in his footprints, praying to know and do God's will, realizing there will be a stiff cost, yet aware that the sacrifice is transformed into delight as our eyes are opened to the joys of creation and the wonder of intimacy with Christ.

Thank you for sharing in this conversation with me. Visit Assisi one day so you too can walk and pray where I have—and do it with someone or a group of someones you love. Read about Francis; pray his prayers; hang an icon here and there.

And every now and then remember this legendary moment: Francis went into a cave and prayed all day. When he emerged at sunset, Brother Leo asked him, "Did God say anything to you today?" Francis said, "No, nothing." The next day, Francis prayed all day again; when he finished, Leo asked, "Did God say anything to you today?" Francis again said, "No, nothing today."

And so it went for quite a number of days. Then one evening Francis came out of the cave. Out of habit more than anything else, Leo asked, "Did God say anything to you today?" Francis replied, "Yes." Leo's eyes flew open: "He did? What did he say?" Francis said, "God said just one word to me today." Leo asked, "What was it? What did God say?" Francis answered, "God simply said, 'More.'" More. God wanted more of Francis. More of his heart, more of his soul, more of his very self. And if we kneel and pray with Francis, we can be sure, if we listen carefully, that God will say to me and to you, "More."

NOTES

Introduction

1. Arnaldo Fortini, *Francis of Assisi*, trans. Helen Moak (New York: Crossroad, 1981), p. 86.

2. Henri Nouwen, ¡*Gracias!*: *A Latin American Journal* (San Francisco: Harper & Row, 1983), p. 11.

3. See Jacques Dalarun, *The Misadventure of Francis of Assisi: Toward a Historical Use of the Franciscan Legends*, trans. Edward Hagman (Saint Bonaventure: Franciscan Institute, 2002).

Chapter 1: The Will of God

1. Regis J. Armstrong, J.A. Wayne Hellman, and William J. Short eds., *Francis of Assisi: Early Documents*, vol. 2 (New York: New City Press, 2000), p. 228.

2. Regis J. Armstrong, J. A. Wayne Hellman, William J. Short eds., *Francis of Assisi: Early Documents*, vol. 1, (New York: New City Press, 1999), p. 187.

3. Pierre Brunette, *Francis of Assisi and His Conversions*, trans. Paul Lachance and Kathryn Krug (Quincy, Mass.: Franciscan, 1997).

4. *Early Documents*, 1:124; Michael Robson, *St. Francis of Assisi: The Legend and the Life* (London: Geoffrey Chapman, 1997), p. 19.

5. Jean Vanier, *From Brokenness to Community* (New York: Paulist, 1992), p. 16.

6. Robert D. Richardson, *Henry Thoreau: A Life of the Mind* (Berkeley: University of California Press, 1988), p. 282.

7. Henry David Thoreau, *Walden*, p. 42.

8. Nicholas Lash, "Performing the Scriptures," in *Theology on the Way to Emmaus* (London: SPCK, 1986), pp. 37–46.

9. Jon M. Sweeney, *The St. Francis Prayer Book: A Guide to Deepen Your Spiritual Life* (Brewster: Paraclete, 2004), pp. 125–26.

Chapter 2: The Value of Possessions

1. Joan Mueller, *The Privilege of Poverty: Clare of Assisi, Agnes of Prague, and the Struggle for a Franciscan Rule for Women* (University Park: Pennsylvania State University Press, 2006), p. 2.

2. *Early Documents*, 1:220.

3. Murray Bodo, *The Way of St. Francis: The Challenge of Franciscan Spirituality for Everyone* (New York: Image, 1984), p. 20.

4. *Early Documents*, 2:89.

5. *Early Documents*, 1:218.

6. Ibid., p. 466.

7. Paul Sabatier, *The Road to Assisi*, ed. Jon M. Sweeney (Brewster: Paraclete, 2003), p. 64.

8. *The Little Flowers, Legends, and Lauds*, ed. Otto Karrer, trans. N. Wydenbruck (London: Sheed & Ward, 1947), p. 161.

9. Murray Bodo, *Juniper: Friend of Francis, Fool of God* (Cincinnati: St. Anthony Messenger, 1983), p. 28.

10. Marilynne Robinson, *Gilead* (New York: Farrar, Straus, Giroux, 2004), p. 31.

11. Claus Westermann, *Genesis 37–50*, trans. John J. Scullion (Minneapolis: Augsburg, 1986), p. 37.

12. Walter Brueggemann, *Genesis* (Atlanta: John Knox, 1982), p. 315.

13. G. K. Chesterton, *St. Francis of Assisi* (Garden City, N.Y.: Image, 1957), pp. 101–103.

14. Bodo, *The Way of St. Francis*, p. 57.

15. Mother Teresa, *My Life for the Poor*, ed. José Luis González-Balado and Janet N. Playfoot (San Francisco: Harper & Row, 1985), pp. 78–79.

16. Jürgen Moltmann, *The Source of Life: The Holy Spirit and the Theology of Life*, trans. Margaret Kohl (Minneapolis: Fortress, 1997), p. 109.

Chapter 3: The Dilemma of Family

1. *Early Documents*, 2:74.

2. Ibid., p. 80.

3. Charles Dickens, *Bleak House*, "telescopic philanthropy" being the title of chapter 4.

4. Bodo, *The Way of St. Francis*, p. 55.

5. *Early Documents*, 2:37.

6. Ibid., p. 82.

7. Nicholas Wolterstorff, *Lament for a Son* (Grand Rapids: Eerdmans, 1987), pp. 64–65.

8. *Early Documents*, 1:182.

9. Lawrence S. Cunningham, *Francis of Assisi: Performing the Gospel Life* (Grand Rapids: Eerdmans, 2004), p. 6.

10. *Early Documents*, 1:429.

11. *The Confessions of St. Augustine* 1.11.17, trans. John K. Ryan (Garden City, N.Y.: Image, 1960), p. 54.

12. *Early Documents*, 1:192.

13. Brunette, *Francis of Assisi and His Conversions*, p. xv.

14. Bodo, *The Way of St. Francis*, p. 57.

15. *Early Documents*, 1:49.

16. Ibid., p. 122.

17. L. Gregory Jones, "Our Children's Happiness," in *Everyday Matters: Intersections of Life and Faith* (Nashville: Abingdon, 2003), pp. 99–102.

Chapter 4: The Smallness of the Church

1. Edwin Mullins, *Cluny: In Search of God's Lost Empire* (New York: Bluebridge, 2006), pp. 173–174.

2. Some say he was baptized in San Giorgio, others in Santa Maria Maggiore (Linda Bird Francke, *On the Road with Francis of Assisi: A Timeless Journey Through Umbria and Tuscany, and Beyond* [New York: Random House, 2005], p. 10); many tours point to the font in San Rufino, the cathedral partially under reconstruction when Francis was born.

3. Karl Barth, *Dogmatics in Outline*, trans. G. T. Thompson (New York: Harper & Row, 1959), pp. 144–45.

4. W. H. Vanstone, *Love's Endeavour, Love's Expense: The Response of Being to the Love of God* (London: Darton Longman Todd, 1977), p. 109.

5. Lawrence S. Cunningham, in *Francis of Assisi: History, Hagiography and Hermeneutics in the Early Documents*, ed. Jay M. Hammond (Hyde Park, New York: New City, 2004), p. 165.

6. Simone Weil, *Waiting for God*, trans. Emma Craufurd (New York: Harper Colophon, 1951), p. 67.

7. *Early Documents*, 1:77.

8. Earlier accounts indicate the meeting with the pope was set up in advance by Bishop Guido and Cardinal John of St. Paul, but later accounts dramatize his arrival as more spontaneous; see Robson, *St. Francis of Assisi* (1997), pp. 73–77.

9. *Early Documents*, 1:63–64. In a letter to Leo near the end of his life, Francis reiterated this theme of following in the footprints (*vestigii*) of Christ.

10. Ibid., p. 64.

11. Jonathan S. Campbell, *The Way of Jesus* (San Francisco: Jossey-Bass, 2005), p. 39.

12. Simone Weil, *Waiting for God*, pp. 67–68.

13. Ulrich Luz, *Matthew in History: Interpretation, Influence, and Effects* (Minneapolis: Fortress, 1994), pp. 40, 45.

Chapter 5: Reading the Bible Literally

1. *Early Documents*, 1:459–60.

2. Nicholas Lash, "Performing the Scriptures," pp. 37–46.

3. Cunningham, in *History, Hagiography and Hermeneutics in the Early Documents*, ed. Hammond, p. 175.

4. *Early Documents*, 1:202.

5. Sabatier, *The Road to Assisi*, p. 118.

6. Cunningham, *Francis of Assisi: Performing the Gospel Life*, p. 125. Giles lamented that "Paris destroyed Assisi" (Robson, *St. Francis of Assisi*, p. 182); and we also have the harsh critique by Jacopone of Todi: "In sorrow and grief I see Paris destroy Assisi stone by stone. With all their theology they've led the Order down a crooked path" (Cunningham, *Francis of Assisi: Performing the Gospel Life*, p. 126).

7. See Dalarun, *The Misadventure of Francis of Assisi*, p. 255; Etienne Gilson, *The Philosophy of Saint Bonaventure* (New York: Sheed and Ward, 1938), pp. 81–82.

8. See Dalarun, *The Misadventure of Francis of Assisi*, p. 250.

9. Rowan Williams, *Where God Happens: Discovering Christ in One Another* (Boston: New Seeds, 2005), p. 147.

10. *Early Documents*, 1:107.

Chapter 6: The Imitation of Christ

1. Picking up on the framework of Frances Young, *Virtuoso Theology: The Bible and Interpretation* (Cleveland: Pilgrim, 1993), see

Cunningham, "Francis Naked and Clothed," in *History, Hagiography and Hermeneutics in the Early Documents*, ed. Hammond, p. 174.

2. Regis J. Armstrong, J. A. Wayne Hellman, and William J. Short eds., *Francis of Assisi: Early Documents*, vol. 3 (New York: New City Press, 2001), p. 566.

3. Ibid., p. 578.

4. *Early Documents*, 1:283.

5. Charles Wesley, "Love Divine, All Loves Excelling," 1747.

6. Albert Schweitzer, *The Quest of the Historical Jesus* (Baltimore: Johns Hopkins University Press, 1998), p. 4.

7. George Marshall and David Poling, *Schweitzer: A Biography* (Baltimore: Johns Hopkins University Press, 2000), p. 49.

8. Ibid., p. 56.

9. *Early Documents*, 1:254.

10. G. K. Chesterton, *St. Francis of Assisi* (Garden City: Image, 1957), 117–18.

11. *The Beatitudes for Today* (Louisville: Westminster John Knox, 2006).

12. Chesterton, *St. Francis of Assisi*, pp. 40, 47.

13. John Chrysostom, "Homilies on the Gospel of St. Matthew," in *Nicene and Post-Nicene Fathers*, ed. Philip Schaff, vol. 10 (Edinburgh: T. & T. Clark, 1991), p. 473.

14. *Early Documents*, 2:148.

15. Sabatier, *The Road to Assisi*, p. 18.

16. Michael Robson, *St. Francis of Assisi: The Legend and the Life* (London: Geoffrey Chapman, 1997), p. 224.

17. "The Legend of the Three Companions," in *The Little Flowers, Legends and Lauds: St. Francis of Assisi*, p. 27.

18. Michael Robson, *St. Francis of Assisi: The Legend and the Life* (London: Geoffrey Chapman, 1997), p. 190.

19. *Early Documents*, 1:254.

20. *St. Francis of Assisi: Writings and Early Biographies; English Omnibus of the Sources for the Life of St. Francis*, ed. Marion Habig, trans. Raphael Brown (Chicago: Franciscan Herald Press, 1973), p. 1448.

21. A comprehensive study by one inclined to skepticism is Ian Wilson, *Stigmata: An Investigation into the Mysterious Appearance of Christ's Wounds in Hundreds of People from Medieval Italy to Modern America* (New York: Harper & Row, 1989).

'22. Francke, *On the Road with Francis of Assisi*, p. 199.

23. *Early Documents*, 3:458–59.

Chapter 7: Peace for Creation and Humanity

1. Quoted and discussed beautifully by Hammond in *Francis of Assisi: History, Hagiography and Hermeneutics in the Early Documents*, p. 138.

2. Cunningham, *Francis of Assisi: Performing the Gospel Life*, p. 99.

3. The previous scriptures from Philippians appear in order as follows: 1:3 KJV; 1:12 NIV; 1:19 RSV; 1:20 RSV; 2:1-2 RSV; 2:17 RSV; 3:8 RSV; 4:4-5 RSV; 4:11 RSV.

4. Roger D. Sorrell, *St. Francis of Assisi and Nature* (New York: Oxford University Press, 1988), p. 71.

5. Chiara Frugoni, *Francis of Assisi: A Life* (New York: Continuum, 1999), p. 13.

6. *Early Documents*, 1:234.

7. *Early Documents*, 3:593.

8. Ibid., 3:632–33.

9. Thomas Merton, *New Seeds of Contemplation* (New York: New Directions, 1961), pp. 29, 31.

10. *Early Documents*, 3:363.

11. *Little Flowers, Legends and Lauds*, p. 164.

12. Gerard Thomas Straub, *The Sun and Moon Over Assisi: A Personal Encounter with Francis and Clare* (Cincinnati: St. Anthony Messenger, 2000), p. 62.

13. Münster Gesangbuch, "Fairest Lord Jesus," 1677. Trans. Joseph August Seiss, 1873.

14. Sorrell, *St. Francis of Assisi and Nature*, p. 139.

15. *Early Documents*, 3:173.

16. Cunningham, *Francis of Assisi: Performing the Gospel Life*, p. 100.

17. Ibid.

18. *Early Documents*, 1:255.

19. Frugoni, *Francis of Assisi*, p. 115.

20. *Early Documents*, 3:602.

21. Carlo Carretto, *I, Francis*, trans. Robert R. Barr (Maryknoll, N.Y.: Orbis, 1982), pp. 75, 80.

22. *Early Documents*, 3:610.

23. Ibid., p. 606.

24 . Dietrich Bonhoeffer, *No Rusty Swords*, trans. John Bowden, ed. Edwin Robertson (New York: Harper & Row, 1956), p. 168, discussed probingly by Stanley Hauerwas, *Performing the Faith: Bonhoeffer and the Practice of Nonviolence* (Grand Rapids: Brazos, 2004), pp. 13–72.

25. Chesterton, *St. Francis of Assisi*, pp. 40, 47.

26. *Early Documents*, 1:245.

27. Bodo, *The Way of St. Francis*, p. 15.

28. Jonathan Sacks, *The Dignity of Difference: How to Avoid the Clash of Civilizations* (London: Continuum, 2003), p. 5.

29. Cunningham, *Francis of Assisi: Performing the Gospel Life*, p. 111.

Conclusion

1. Leonardo Boff, *Saint Francis: A Model for Human Liberation*, trans. John W. Diercksmeier (New York: Crossroad, 1989), p. 21.

2. Gerard Thomas Straub, *Sun and Moon Over Assisi*, p. 128.